EMERALD GUIDES

EMERALD GUIDES

GUIDE TO UNDERSTANDING DEPRESSION

NICOLETTE HEATON-HARRIS

Emerald Publishing
www.emeraldpublishing.co.uk

EMERALD GUIDES
Brighton BN2 4EG

ISBN 1847160 47 6
ISBN 13: 9781847160 47 8

Printed by Biddles Ltd Kings Lynn Norfolk

Cover design by Bookworks Islington

Essex County Council Libraries

Dedication:

For my Mum and all those people whose diagnosis of depression is delayed because they spend so much time putting on a brave face for the rest of the world.

Contents

Foreword

Authors Acknowledgements

Index

Foreword

Each and every one of us experiences times in our day to day lives, when we feel 'down' or a 'little blue'. These times can be the result of anything small or significant occurring, depending upon the type of character we are. For example, an upsetting phone call from a relative, a bad day at work, a harsh commute, the end of a relationship or simply turmoil in our own homes.

This 'blue' mood may make us feel a little lethargic for a while. We may feel like we can't be bothered to try and put things right, we may even have a little cry to get the upset out of our systems. We may discover our sleep gets disturbed on one or two nights or we may comfort ourselves with food.

But after a while these feelings pass.

We slowly return to 'normal'.

This is not considered depression, even if you do say to colleagues or friends that you 'felt' depressed for a while. This relatively short experience is described as having a low mood.

Depression on the other hand, usually lasts for two weeks or more.

Constantly.

And it also has greater effects on the sufferer. Unfortunately, the symptoms are many and varied and can be missed or mistaken for some other medical condition.

But put simply, if you have a low mood that lasts continuously for more than a fortnight and you have a real hardship just to simply get through each day, then you must visit a GP for a thorough assessment and medical check-up.

Depression will not go away on its own. You cannot stick your head in the sand like the proverbial ostrich and hope everything gets better without your input. It takes more than just being able to pull yourself together.

Depression is not a weakness. It does not make you any less of a man or a woman because you suffer from it. It's a very common condition, affecting one in five adults during their lifetime.

If you're reading this book, then I'm going to assume you've already been diagnosed by your doctor, or you at least strongly suspect that you have this condition. If so, let's take a good long look at what is ailing you.

Knowledge is power, and by knowing what you are up against, it will arm you in the fight ahead to regain your health.

It can be beaten.

1

WHAT IS DEPRESSION?

Depression is not a static condition that is the same for every sufferer. It is a rapidly changing animal, in a constant flux, affecting different people in different ways.

However, this does not mean that the symptoms cannot be reported. There are general patterns and doctors can be signposted by descriptions or certain words you use when you see them to tell them how you've been feeling. They note these 'red flags' of warning and come to a diagnosis.

You have depression. But what is it? And what is it not?

FACTS

- Anyone of any age can suffer with depression
- More women than men are affected
- One in five adults will suffer with depression in their lifetime**
- Every year, doctors diagnose two million new cases in the UK alone
- On average, each GP in the UK will see one depressive patient a day
- Depression can be treated effectively

---

* As quoted from "The British Medical Association Family Doctor Guide to Depression" by Dr Kwame McKenzie (2000, Dorling Kindersley)

13

- It is not a weakness of the mind
- Rates of depression have increased over the last few decades
- Stress is greatly related to depression

Where you live may greatly affect your chances of suffering with depression. Dwellers of inner cities who live in a hustle-bustle world are twice as likely to suffer with it as those people who live in the remoter parts of the country. So if you live in, for example, London, and you have what you consider a 'normal' life, you are still twice as more likely to suffer with depression than someone who lives in the country, simply because of your geographical location. So in this example, your risk factor of having depression, is nothing to do with you as a person, whether you have a confident manner, or not. It is out of your hands and down to the place you live in.

Depression comes in two distinct forms - reactive and endogenous. Reactive depression comes about because of an event in that sufferer's life. Eg, the birth of a baby, redundancy, long illness, bereavement, etc. Whereas endogenous depression means it has come from within and appears to be for no obvious reason, except for chemical changes within the body and brain.

Depression can show itself in two distinct ways.

Psychologically and physically.

Some of the psychological symptoms may be a result of the physical symptoms and vice versa. Sometimes the physical symptoms aren't even noticed because the psychological symptoms are so bad. So if you do suspect you have depression and have not yet been to your doctor, try to make a note of everything that you feel is wrong with you, as it may well all be connected.

PSYCHOLOGICAL SYMPTOMS OF DEPRESSION

- Not all sufferers of depression will report 'feeling low'
- You may feel constantly anxious
- Emotionally numb (feel you have no mood changes at all)
- Low mood
- Persistent feeling of sadness
- Feeling empty
- A sense of loss or dread
- A low mood worse in the morning (Diurnal Variation)
- Nothing seems to bring any pleasure (Anhedonia)
- Low mood may seem worse in the evenings
- The odd good day, outnumbered by the bad
- Crying more often from slight or even no upset
- Depressive thinking
- Concentration and memory problems
- Delusions
- Hallucinations
- Suicidal impulse

As you can see, psychological symptoms are all those symptoms classed as happening in your mind.

PHYSICAL SYMPTOMS OF DEPRESSION

- Difficulty with sleeping (getting to sleep/waking too early/sleeping too much)
- Mental and physical slowing
- Increase or decrease in appetite
- Increase or decrease in weight
- Problems with libido
- Tiredness and lethargy, aches and pains
- Constipation
- Problems with the menstrual cycle

Here, physical problems come from what is happening to the body.

I'm now going to take a more in-depth look at some of these symptoms, so see if you feel that they match some of your own. If they do, then make sure that you mention them to your doctor.

ANXIETY

Anxiety is a generalised, pervasive fear of something known or unknown, however in the case of depression, the anxiety is usually of an unknown source. Physically, when we feel anxious, our bodies create adrenaline and extra blood is sent to the brain and our muscles throughout our body for 'flight or fight'.

We feel edgy. Tense. But, if nothing dangerous occurs, this feeling passes and we begin to relax, yet if you have depression, this anxious feeling of being constantly on edge can last for months. It can be exhausting in itself.

You wake up in the mornings already in a high state of dread and this in turn, can make you irritable. You may snap at those close to you that you love, upsetting others as well as yourself, leading to other feelings of guilt. This anxiety can make you nervous. Indecisive. It can make you second guess your every decision and debate your self-worth because you just don't know what to do for the best. Therefore the anxiety adds to the depression and becomes a vicious cycle.

(Lizzie's Story : "I had the worst anxiety when I suffered with depression. I was in university and living away from my family and trying to cope with these huge workloads of study. I doubted my ability to cope and I got into the habit of biting my nails so much they would bleed. Seeing the blood frightened me at first, but then it made me feel better. It was like I was finding an outlet valve for the pressure inside of me and so I started to find other ways of making myself bleed. Small cuts at first. Then bigger ones. The more I hid it from everyone the bigger a secret it became. I felt ashamed of myself and felt a fraud.")

EMOTIONALLY NUMB
Some severely depressed people may say that they feel emotionally numb.

There are no highs or lows for them. Everything is constant. Nothing inspires an emotional response and they cannot even cry. They may say they feel that there is nothing inside of them to give, making the sufferer feel that they are completely separate from family and friends.

DEPRESSIVE THINKING

How you think changes dramatically when you have depression. A sufferer can view the world around them in a completely negative light, which reinforces their initial thoughts. They do not see good things happening. They only focus on the bad and make mountains out of molehills.

(Ebony's Story : " I suffer with depression quite badly, though I still work as a secretary in a law firm. I find it real hard to see anything positive from my day. Yesterday my boss asked me to type out some letters he'd dictated, which I did. There were five to do and they needed to be done by the end of the day. When he went to sign them, he spotted a spelling mistake and nicely asked me to make sure it was corrected before it got sent out. That was it. That was all I could think of. That one spelling mistake. It ruined my day. I felt incompetent and totally useless at my job. I almost thought of quitting. I didn't see that I'd got four letters right, nor that I'd got them finished really quickly to get them in the last post. It was the bad thing that mattered most of all.")

CONCENTRATION AND MEMORY PROBLEMS

When a sufferer is in a state of depression, it can be hard to focus on anything within their world. Anyone who needs to remember facts needs to be able to concentrate, so if you suffer with depression, your memory can also be poor. You become indecisive or inattentive. You don't listen well or you get muddled by instructions and confused. Again, it becomes a vicious circle. (An elderly sufferer of depression with this symptom may have it misdiagnosed as the start of dementia.)

DELUSIONS AND HALLUCINATIONS

These severe symptoms usually only occur if a person is severely depressed. Their mind begins to lose touch with reality. It can play tricks. Or, at least, it seems to. A patient may fear they are going mad. Hallucinations and delusions are rare in depression. The hallucinations may manifest themselves as false images, sounds or voices, whereas delusions manifest themselves as false beliefs.

SUICIDAL IMPULSE

When hit by a severe bout of depression, all of a person's life may appear to be awful, without hope for the future and full of past mistakes. The present may seem pointless and incredibly painful to be in. A person may find themselves wondering if life is worth living?

Considering committing suicide may be a passing thought and can be quickly dismissed, but if you were to reach even this point, then you must get yourself help urgently. Help can be through your GP, a doctor in an Accident & Emergency, the Samaritans, or even just a very close, concerned friend who could arrange the help for you, if you feel unable to do it yourself. Remember, depression is treatable.

Continuing thoughts of suicide are alarming and dangerous and you will need help to get yourself through such a dark time. Tell someone. But get yourself help. Because no-one needs to end their life because of depression.

PHYSICAL SYMPTOMS OF DEPRESSION

Some depressive cases may present themselves with physical symptoms only and make them harder to spot. A sufferer may believe that they have something physical wrong with them. However, doctors are trained to spot these cases, too. Some of these physical symptoms that may manifest themselves, are explained below.

SLEEP PROBLEMS

These kinds of problems are common in depression and vary in their form. A sufferer may present with the inability to get to sleep. Or they may present with the fact that they sleep too much. A patient may feel tired and sleepy all day, yawning constantly or they may find that when they do sleep, their sleep is disturbed. They toss and turn and constantly wake to check the clock. Others may wake extremely early or have a combination of these symptoms.

MENTAL AND PHYSICAL SLOWING

Sometimes, a patient may say to their doctor that they feel they are constantly moving through treacle. Their bodies feel like they are seizing up from the inside and struggling to carry out everyday tasks. They're tired, their muscles ache, despite taking painkillers. Everything for them is such an effort to do. They feel like they're living in a slow-motion world. They might even talk slowly, it's such an effort. Movements are slow (psychomotor retardation), their mouth is dry constantly, they get constipated or their periods have stopped/become irregular. They may worry that physically, they have something seriously wrong with them.

LOSS OF APPETITE

A depressed person may lose some weight through loss of

appetite and without eating a nutritional, balanced diet, may leave themselves open to infection or ill health. Interest in food is at an all-time low and when they do eat, the food tastes bland and uninteresting. If their mouth is dry, they may have difficulty chewing and swallowing the food. They may not feel like bothering with meals at all. Or a sufferer may simply never feel hungry. Then as their bodies run on no fuel at all, they become tired and lethargic. It can all become a vicious circle that seems impossible to sort.

REVERSE PHYSICAL SYMPTOMS

Of all of the these symptoms above, a few depressive sufferers may find that they are affected by the exact reverse of the problems. They may overeat, sleep too much, gain large amounts of weight or be hyperactive. In any of these cases, it is imperative to be seen by a GP.

OTHER PHYSICAL SYMPTOMS

Depression can cause plenty of other physical symptoms in a sufferer such as generalised aches and pains, sore joints, feeling pressure in the head, the face, the spine, chest or stomach.

SEX

Perhaps one of the most physical symptoms of depression is an effect on libido, the sexual drive. Many depressed patients feel that they have no interest in sex with their partner. This can be caused not only by the actual physical disinterest, but also can be affected if the sufferer feels generally numb about the world. That they have no highs or lows, so why bother with sex? If they're agitated, they may experience an inability to relax or in the case of a man, get and maintain an erection. Women feel they cannot be aroused, or that intercourse is painful and their bodies are unable to respond in the normal way. Some sufferers may feel that they are just totally unable to say why they don't want to be intimate. Lack of libido can cause great problems and issues in a relationship, so an abrupt change in libido would certainly be cause to consult a doctor.

WHAT CAN CAUSE THESE SYMPTOMS?
So what causes depression? And all these symptoms, whether physical or mental? It's certainly a complicated cocktail of chemicals and hormones, balance and measure. And to understand how this might affect any of us, we must have a basic understanding of how our brains work.

The human brain, whether male or female, is made of billions of nerve cells. Hundreds, if not thousands of these nerve cells are utilised to carry out a single action, whether it's the eyes blinking, or simply just having a thought.

For these nerve cells to work properly and efficiently they need to be able to communicate with each other and to do this, they release a special chemical called a neurotransmitter, from the ends of themselves into spaces between the cells. These spaces are called synapses.

Nerve cell releases

Neurotransmitter into the synapse space which sends message to next nerve cell. In the brain, there are actually different types of neurotransmitters, most importantly, noradrenaline, serotonin and dopamine. You may have heard of any of these.

**[Noradrenaline (norepinephrine) is a hormone closely related to adrenaline, with similar actions. It is secreted by the medulla (the inner area) of the adrenal gland. Its many jobs are the constriction of small blood vessels, leading to an increase in blood pressure, increased blood flow through the coronary arteries and a slowing of the heart rate, increase in the rate and depth of breathing and relaxation of the smooth muscle in the intestinal wall. Serotonin (5-hydroxytryptamine) is vastly distributed in the central nervous system, the intestinal wall and in the blood platelets. Serotonin is used in the treatment of migraines and its levels in the brain are a great influence on mood. Drugs that have serotonin as its heart, are utilised widely in the treatment of depression in the form of anti-depressants. Dopamine acts on certain dopamine receptors and also on adrenergic receptors throughout the body especially in the extrapyramidal system of the brain and in the heart's arteries. Dopamine also stimulates the release of noradrenaline from nerve endings. These three neurotransmitters will be in short supply if person is suffering with depression. The synapses are low in these important chemicals, leading to a breakdown in communication and faulty connections of messages, directly causing depressive symptoms. When a doctor prescribes you anti-depressants, they are increasing the levels of these chemicals and your neurotransmitters to assist in normal brain communication.

---

* As quoted from "The Oxford Concise Medical Dictionary" edited by Elizabeth E. Martin MA (2003, OUP)

THE ROLE OF HORMONES

Hormones are equally to blame in causing the symptoms of depression. The hormone adrenaline, in high quantities, can cause anxiety. Cortisol is our bodies reaction to stress.

Cortisol is a steroid hormone and when we are stressed, we release amounts of it into our body from the adrenal cortex, causing alterations in our immune reactions, our kidney function and effects the levels of fats and sugars in our blood supply. The control of the release of cortisol is in the pituitary gland of the brain. If a person is healthy, a large amount of cortisol is released into the body in the morning, allowing it to diminish throughout the rest of the day. But if a person is depressed, a large amount of cortisol is released all day long and as you can see from the above information, this one hormone alone could cause significant changes in our body and mood.

2

POST-NATAL DEPRESSION

The birth of a new baby is meant to be such a joyous time for all involved. But for many women, the first couple of years after their child's birth is a time they feel they would rather forget. They also feel anger, especially afterwards, because they feel that they have missed out on their babies' first weeks, months or years. They worry about whether they bonded correctly. Whether their child loves them.

Because they suffered with post-natal depression.

There are many different types of depression, all with differing symptoms, as I described briefly in the last chapter, but only this depression can be categorised because of one same event in a person's life.

The birth of their baby.

And I mention 'their' baby, because lately, it has also been speculated that it is not only women who can suffer with post-natal depression. However, the majority of the public at large, only think of mothers as suffering, despite their usually being a couple involved in bringing a child into the world. Therefore, this section will mainly concentrate on the mothers.

It has also been argued, that post-natal depression does not start after the birth of a baby, but can actually begin long before that, during the pregnancy, or even pre-conceptually.

There are three main types of depression associated with the time after birth and I will go into each of them here. The first is known as the 'baby-blues'.

THE BABY BLUES.

The baby blues is known by many names and typically seems to affect mothers at around the time their milk comes in, three days after giving birth. It is thought that these 'blues', which are only temporary, are caused by the vast amounts of hormones at work in the body. Hormones needed to produce the milk for the baby to feed from. The levels of oestrogen and progesterone drop dramatically after birth and it is thought that half of all new mothers experience the 'baby blues'.

The baby blues is not so much a 'depressive state', rather a period of low mood.

(Personally, I can remember the first time I experienced baby blues, after the birth of my first son. I was at home, feeling fine, when my husband gave me a wallet of photographs containing all the new photos he'd taken of our new son. Pictures taken of us both in hospital. Me looking exhausted, but happy and our son, cradled in the arms of various people. Suddenly, it all seemed so much to take in. The baby I'd wanted for so long was here. It was a boy, the first grandson on my husband's side of the family and I just felt so out of it. I burst into tears, astounding my husband, who thought he'd make me happy by then presenting me with a beautiful diamond eternity ring. This just made me cry all the more and that was how I was for about two days. Crying at the slightest thing. The news upset me. Silly adverts. NSPCC commercials. Forget it. I was exhausted, tired, I needed to sleep, my whole body ached and my head felt like someone was trying to do the washing up in it. Strangely, I don't recall suffering with baby blues after the birth of my twins when I was stuck in hospital for five days after a caesarean, nor after the birth of my third son when I got sent home the very next day.)

However, this low mood is not unique to first time mothers. So what is needed, if anything, to help a mother with the baby blues?

Any woman suffering with low mood during the first week after giving birth, needs emotional support. Her partner, if she has one, can help her with whatever she needs, whether she just needs a nice cup of tea after feeding the baby or the offer of having someone run them a bath. Allow a new mother to have as much sleep as she can during the day and if she can time it for when the baby is sleeping, then so much the better. Family can help out by cooking meals or taking care of the house or if the parents are okay with it, perhaps taking the baby out for a walk in its pram, allowing the new parents a brief respite, or time to be with their other children. However, it is also worth noting that there can sometimes be a very fine line to be trod here. Offers of help will be appreciated. Taking over everything, will not.

Always ask the mother if she minds, because no-one wants to make her feel worthless or useless, especially if she had a difficult birth and is still in some considerable pain. Mothers today put an awful lot of pressure on themselves to be perfect and so expect to be able to look after things for themselves when they get home and sometimes this cannot be the case. Especially if a caesarean section was the method of delivery. No-one wants the 'baby blues' to become something a lot more difficult to get through.

POST-NATAL DEPRESSION
Statistics state that fifteen out of every one hundred mothers will experience post-natal depression.

At one time, it was thought to be lower than this, as it is very hard to notice sometimes, but recently, health visitors now give out questionnaires to new mothers when they see them ten to eleven days after delivery, to assess their emotional and mental state.

However, this kind of depression is quite easily treated after it has been diagnosed.

Once the initial elation of a birth has passed, visitors are no longer calling and the father (if there is one) has returned to work, the mother gets left alone to care for the baby. For some women, this is okay. Difficult and tiring, yes, but they manage. Some might even admit to thriving at it. Yet for some women, this is a time when they are at risk for getting deeper into depression.

They're alone. They feel unsupported. Isolated. There seems to be an awful lot of responsibility to care for their baby and they haven't had much sleep. And what sleep they have had, has been of the disturbed variety. Anxiety sets in. Worry. They fret about what they are doing and begin to neglect themselves in favour of doing everything for their child. But then they get exhausted. They're perhaps still in a little pain. They're still bleeding after the birth and they feel drained. They've still got to cook and clean and shop and wash and eventually something has to give. An innocent comment from a strange admirer in the street can be devastating. The mother worries some more, her anxiety levels rise, her exhaustion gets worse as she tries to make everything right and when she tries to tell her partner about it, she feels he doesn't listen, or he shrugs her worries off as nothing. She keeps things to herself and agonises over them. She begins to feel there is nothing else in her life but the baby. Fun? What's that? Laughter? Who's got time to laugh about anything, can't you see the baby has only put on an ounce in weight and the health visitor said she was small?

Guilt sets in and she may feel that secretly, everyone is criticising her or thinking she is a bad mother or worse, useless. She may start snapping at her partner, her other children. She may become highly irritable.

This can't all be down to just hormones because then every woman who has a child would suffer from it.

Post-natal depression has its roots in genetics too and perhaps to some degree, the social factors surrounding an individual. We've already learnt that where you live can have some affect on your mindset.

So what factors might put you more at risk of suffering post-natal depression than someone else?

- o If the problems start before the birth and the whole process has been one long one of trying to get pregnant. Maybe having some fertility problems and needing medical assistance to start the process.
- o If you have other worries in life, such as the state of your finances and the pregnancy wasn't planned. You're worried about how you'll cope.

o If you're aware that any of your relatives have had depression or mental illness and that it seems to be quite prevalent in your family.

o If you're a single parent and doing it all alone.

o If you're not completely sure whether you want the baby or not and it happens to be a very difficult child. Crying constantly.

o If the baby had medical problems. Perhaps it was premature or has a genetic defect. What is that child's future? You think 'Was there anything I could have done better?'

o If you had a difficult pregnancy and birth. If you were separated from your baby.

o If you have to return to work after the birth, but feel you have been given a different job. Something easier, or you feel you've been demoted. Problems with childcare and fitting everything in. You have to work you need the money to live...

o If you have suffered with post-natal depression before.

As you can clearly see, there are a lot of implications and lots to think about when a new child comes into the world and it affects everyone. Dads too. They feel that suddenly they have a lot of extra responsibility. They want to provide for their partner and child/children, but feel they're working themselves into the ground. Then they come home and their partner is upset after a difficult day and he feels the need to take care of her too, leaving no time for himself. His sleep is also disturbed, yet public expectations are that 'men can cope', he tells no-one about how he feels because he thinks he may seem less of a man, and he bottles it all up inside.

The father gets post-natal depression and no-one notices because the focus is all on the mother. He then feels isolated and unsupported. You can understand why it is such a vicious circle.

Treating post-natal depression is usually quite successful, especially if caught in its early stages.

A combination of Cognitive Behaviour Therapy (CBT) and anti-depressants seem to be the most popular methods used and anti-depressants have the benefit of being able to be taken whilst a mother is still breast-feeding. Women treated for post-natal depression can soon feel better, whilst those who try to soldier through without benefit of treatment, usually don't see any improvement in themselves until after their child starts walking and talking.

SEVERE POST-NATAL DEPRESSION / PUERPURAL PSYCHOSIS

This is a much rarer kind of depression, unique and unusual, affecting a mother mostly within the first fortnight after giving birth. (When it is seen in women, it is noted that the majority have had psychiatric problems before pregnancy.)

The difference in symptoms from a classic depressive state and puerpural psychosis, is that if suffering with the latter, a woman may lose touch with reality, experiencing frequent delusions and hallucinations. The delusions may take the form of the belief that there is something seriously wrong with the baby or seriously wrong with herself and any added

31

hallucinations may pose a severe risk to the health and safety of the baby and/or the mother.

Some mothers suffering with puerpural psychosis have been known to kill their babies, believing it is for the best. That they are putting the child out of its perceived misery.

In this situation (which is treatable) it is usually best to treat the mother whilst in hospital or a specialised unit. There, she may remain in contact with her child, but will have supervision and help from staff who are trained in these situations. Anti-depressants are usually given and any other medication which is needed to treat any hallucinations and/or delusions the mother may be experiencing. She will also be counselled and receive therapy, especially before she is released back home. Check-ups will be strongly advised.

The mother will still be allowed to breastfeed whilst on anti-depressants, but if she is given other medications to help with her other issues, then any of these may pass into the breast milk and a decision will have to be made about continuing with breast-feeding. (eg; Lithium can affect babies). Any woman who suffers with post-natal depression, severe or otherwise, will be at risk of developing it again after or before future pregnancies. If you are planning on having another child and have already experienced depression or post-natal depression, then please make sure you inform your doctor and midwife, so that they can make a note of it in your record. This way you will be carefully monitored when you have your next child and receive early, beneficial treatment.

Post-natal depression is not a condition that needs to be hidden from anyone you consider to be in authority. They will not take your child away from you. They will not consider you an unfit mother and bring social services into your life, like some women may believe.

It is treatable. And the help is out there.

Do not be afraid to ask for it.

Gemma's* Story

Our problems started with conception. We couldn't get pregnant and eventually we were referred to IVF. Our first three attempts failed and after each cycle and horrendous negative result, I'd swear I'd never do it again. The pressure on Mark*, too, was awful and we'd bicker and fight about most things.

I could feel I was getting depressed. Sinking lower and lower into some abyss that I just couldn't get out of, but to everyone else I seemed fine! I was happy, smiling Gemma! 'Nothing can get that girl down', they'd say. Well, they were wrong.

Eventually, we felt able to try a fourth time and thank God, it was successful! They'd inserted two embryos and one took. We paid for extra scans throughout the pregnancy, just to make sure everything was fine and Mark had me wrapped in cotton wool. Anything I wanted, he'd get. Nothing was too much trouble. I was really happy and enjoyed my pregnancy. The darkness had gone. I was pregnant, what more did I need?

But then everything went badly at the birth. I'd written a plan but didn't get anything I wanted. The wards were busy, the midwives were overrun with patients. I was in agony and didn't get my epidural for ages. After labouring for thirty-four hours, I finally reached ten centimetres and I could push, but I didn't do it very well. I was given an episiotomy, which I didn't want, and forceps were used. I felt violated. I was in agony and hating every minute of it. Having a baby was meant to be a good thing. A happy time.

Eventually, Jamie* was born. He was a good weight and healthy and I held him whilst I was stitched up. But then I haemorrhaged badly and needed a blood transfusion. I spent three days in hospital and was then sent home.

Everyone fussed about me and the baby, saying how perfect he was, how lovely. All they wanted to do was see the baby and all I could think of, was 'what about me? What about what I went through? Sod Jamie!'

The guilt I had for those thoughts was immense and I didn't eat very well. Jamie kept me awake most nights feeding constantly and I felt like I'd given birth to a leech. I didn't feel like a mother. I felt like a machine. I was exhausted, sleep-deprived and wasn't enjoying my baby. My health visitor seemed to realise something wasn't right straight away and she took me into another room for a chat whilst Mark looked after Jamie. I can remember bursting into tears and all my thoughts and feelings about everything came pouring out. She arranged for me to see my GP and I got prescribed anti-depressants. They help. They do. But so does talking to Mark about how I feel.

I feel cheated out of those first few days I had with Jamie. I wish I'd said something earlier, in the hospital, but I just felt like all decisions had been taken out of my hands. I was just the mother. The baby was more important. Sound selfish, don't I? But who says anyone thinks straight when they're depressed?

* Names changed

3

MANIC / BI-POLAR DEPRESSION

If you are diagnosed as having manic depression or bi-polar depression, then they are exactly the same thing.

Patients with manic depression are notably different from patients with 'classic' depression, because they have long-lasting highs and then sudden, long-lasting low moods.

If they are on a high, they are described as being 'manic'. These highs are when the patient shows signs of being extremely happy. Everything is right in their world. Money is no object. They are extravagant. Generous. Nothing is too much trouble and they race from one thing to another in a state of high energy. They don't appear to have any real need to sleep or eat. In fact some sufferers don't seem to be aware of any appetite at all and only drink or eat if they are reminded to do so. Inside, they feel great. Healthy. Fit. Their minds race with thoughts and sometimes it may seem that their mouths are unable to keep up with the stream of consciousness running at a high inside their heads. They may make a bad decision, but shrug it off, saying it didn't matter, especially if they are also suffering with hallucinations and delusions, which a few manic-depressives experience. These delusions can seem extreme to others and are often the first clue to bewildered family and friends that something might be wrong.

Then a low mood hits and everything that the patient was in their manic state is the extreme opposite. The patient is incredibly low and depressed. The world seems a bleak place, full of misery and oppression. They worry and fret over tiny things and have no energy to move, wash themselves or keep their eyes open. They might not be able to sleep or find that they can sleep for many hours at a time and wake exhausted. Their minds might feel sluggish and uncooperative and they might experience thoughts of harming themselves. The lows can last for days, then suddenly, they wake from a low episode and find themselves manic again.

This is why manic depression is also called bi-polar. The word bi-polar means 'having two poles or extremities'.

Manic depressives do not seem to recall being in their previous state. In a low mood, they may recall their elated state as being some aberration in their behaviour. Yet if they are manic, they dismiss their low as not being them. They become delusional regarding their low state because whilst they are manic, everything is good.

Manic depression can be controlled by drugs and these have to be taken regularly over a long period of time, to keep control of the manic episodes.

The thing to realise and remember, is that bipolar disorder is a lifelong condition and sometimes very hard to diagnose. During a manic episode, you might feel great, on a high. You wouldn't think of going to a doctor at this time. But when depressed and experiencing your 'low', you might see your GP and be diagnosed as having 'normal' depression, mainly because it won't occur to you to say that you experience highs as well. Because of this, it is important when you see your

GP, that you mention what your moods are like in general and not just right at that particular moment. And if you are unable to do so, then perhaps have someone with you who can help describe what has been going on.

Doctors can help tremendously with bipolar depression. It cannot be cured, but the vast range of the mood swings, from depression to mania, can be stabilised and this medication is something that you will probably have to take for the rest of your life.

You may experience 4 different types of mood swings:

- Depression - when you feel extremely sad and low
- Mania - feeling on a high or even being very irritable, manic and edgy, or performing risky tasks
- Hypomania - a milder type of mania. A generalised 'feel-good' feeling, where you think that you are at last capable of achieving things. That life isn't a problem.
- Mixed mood - when your episodes of mania and depression switch between the two very rapidly.

So you can see why it is important to clearly describe to your GP what you have been like for a while, rather than the last week or so.

OTHER DISORDERS LINKED TO BIPOLAR DEPRESSION

- Eating disorders, such as anorexia nervosa or bulimia
- Attention Deficit Hyperactivity Disorder (ADHD)
- Panic Disorder
- Social Phobia

The four things to remember about bipolar are:
- Bipolar can be managed, not cured
- It is not easy to diagnose
- You can still live your life and keep your job if you take the correct medication
- You must take your medication for life, even if you feel 'better'.

CASE HISTORY - SPIKE MILLIGAN

Born in India in 1918, Spike grew up to serve in the Royal Artillery in World War II. In Italy, he was wounded in action and was hospitalised for shellshock before experiencing his first mental breakdown.

After this, he broke into entertainment with *The Goon Show* and his own *Q* series, but having to write a show a week put immense pressure on him and affected his health in many ways, eventually leading to another breakdown. His doctors decided to treat him with Lithium and whilst feeling depressed, he started writing some serious poetry. Diagnosed with Bi-Polar Disorder, he admitted in his biography to having had 'at least ten breakdowns', several of them lasting a year or more each. He spoke openly about his condition and even wrote a book about it entitled, *Depression, and How To Survive It*.

4

JUVENILE DEPRESSION

I have included this chapter on its own because I believe it deserves its own section, rather than just an addendum, or footnote.

It is unfortunate that in this day and age that young children actually suffer with depression, and many parents/adults do not believe that children are capable of suffering with it.

The term 'juvenile' is restricted to those that are seventeen years of age, or below and sadly, juvenile depression is a lot more common than most people would like to believe, affecting about two in every hundred children before they hit puberty and averaging around nine in every one hundred adolescents. In the teenage years, girls, more than boys, seem to be affected more and there is a distinct lack of enjoyment in activities that they once found pleasurable. They lose their appetite, their sleep patterns are poor and inconsistent. Some gain weight, rather than lose it, as they seek comfort in food high in calories and show an abnormal amount of concern for their own health and wellbeing. Teachers may notice that a child's school performance may drop. There are even some teenagers who think about self-harming, or even harbour thoughts on suicide.

Boys may find it tough, in that they might have been raised not to show their inner feelings and emotions so that they feel they cannot admit to being upset or sad, or feeling the need to cry and therefore show their turmoil instead in extreme acts of irritability or acting bored/being destructive/self-harming.

The difficulties in teenagers suffering with depression and being diagnosed, is that most people will automatically assume that the teenager is simply being hormonal, and therefore 'typical' of being a teenager. Some youngsters, like adults, are not able to cope with the stresses and strains of their everyday life and depression results. They may be unable to cope with:

- Starting a new school
- Making friends
- Being bullied/teased on a day to day basis
- Unable to cope with school work
- Problems in the home, such as marriage break up, having a single parent, having a parent addicted to a substance, abuse, poverty, being fostered, adopted, etc
- Hormonal changes as they approach puberty
- Problems with menstruation
- Long-term illness
- Social issues
- Exam pressures
- A death of a parent or family member

We have already read about in earlier chapters, some of the symptoms of depression, both mental and physical and how they affect us, so imagine how this must feel to a child. An individual, who may be quite young, and without the broad vocabulary necessary to explain just what they feel like. It could be quite easy for their depression to be missed by a parent or a GP. Many people automatically think of young children as being happy and carefree. Why would they suspect depression in a child? And even if that child did show signs of depression and the parent had thoughts along the lines of 'Hm, Jane/John dont seem themselves lately' how many of them would ignore it, assuming that their child was just having a low moment? Something that would soon pass? Perhaps a parent suspects depression, but does not take their child to the doctor because they fear the doctors will blame them?

It has been noted by some researchers, that the earlier the age depression hits, the more family members that child has that have also suffered at some point, or currently have depression also.

Depression in young people is often found to occur alongside other mental health disorders, such as anxiety, being constantly disruptive or abusing illegal substances, or even with the physical disorders such as diabetes.*[1]

Juvenile depression is prevalent these days and it is not

---

[1]   (Angold A, Costello EJ. Depressive Co-Morbidity In

Children And Adolescents: Empirical, Theoretical and

Methodological Issues. American Journal of Psychiatry, 1993;

150 [12]: 1779-91)

an issue to stick our heads in the sand about. So what can you do if you are a parent who suspects your child is depressed? Or you've already taken your child to the doctor?

At your GP's surgery, your doctor may give your child, at first, a physical exam or even take a blood sample to rule out any physical causes. If clear, your doctor may refer your child to the Child and Adolescent Mental Health Service (CAMHS). In this case, you will be contacted by a counsellor who may come to your home first of all to talk to you about what you have noticed about your child's behaviour, and then, if old enough, they will attempt to talk to your child. This can happen either individually, or as a family. Anti-depressants may sometimes be prescribed, though some doctors may be reluctant to prescribe drugs or medications for quite young children. The CAMHS counsellor may involve the school, your child's teacher or school nurse in what is happening and even observe the child at school, if they are still able to attend.

As a parent you need to remember that your child is looking at the world darkly. There isn't much in their lives that is much fun and they may not be feeling anything if they are experiencing emotional numbness. Take each day as it comes and always let them know that you are there for them always. That if they need you, you will come and listen, or talk, or whatever it is that they need from you at that time. Always tell them you love them, no matter what. That you hear what they are saying (even if you don't understand why they are feeling such a way) and that you will do whatever you can to help.

Obviously, this may be difficult if you have more than one child to take care of. Finding the time to involve yourself exclusively with one child is impossible if there are others to care for too, so try and balance yourself.

You may have occasion to take your child to the counsellor's therapy rooms or try different programs, especially if the child is very young and is involved in play therapy or Social Stories. (A series of stories to help children understand situations if they have communication problems such as Semantic Pragmatic Disorder.)

Don't expect any quick fixes with depression.

Most children with depression have the condition for about nine months before treatment begins to alleviate their problems. Usually, by the time a year has passed, up to 90% of sufferers will have recovered. One in ten children will remain persistently depressed and about half will relapse after their recovery.

For details of what the responsibility of school's are in Mental Health Issues, then please visit the website below for more information:

www.teachernet.gov.uk/wholeschool/sen/ypmentalhealth/

(This includes details of CAMHS.)

Claire's* Story

I enjoyed my time at school. I wasn't bullied or anything, though I did get a lot of ribbing from the fact I was Head Girl and most kids called me a swot. Sure, I worked hard. Did my homework, made sure I got things right and I got good results in my mock GCSEs. My parents were thrilled with each result or good comment and would read my school reports all the time. They kept dropping hints. Saying with brains like mine, I could be the first person in our family to go to university and make something of themselves. They even told me they could see me as a doctor or a lawyer, or something. But I didn't want that. I liked animals. I wanted to work in a vets and I told them so. They said, 'great, train to be a vet then', but I didn't want to be a vet. I couldn't see myself putting animals to sleep, I knew I'd get upset. I just wanted to care for them. Maybe train as an animal nurse or something.

Well, my parents went ballistic. Said I was throwing away my one opportunity. My Dad wouldn't speak to me for weeks. My mum refused to help me write letters to vet surgeries asking for jobs or work experience as she said I was letting them all down. The pressure they put on me was huge!

I couldn't sleep. I wasn't really eating. I was hearing nothing back from the vet's surgeries I'd applied to and was beginning to think my parents were right. I'd left school with good GCSEs, but what were they compared to graduates' degrees?

The doctor diagnosed me with nervous depression and put me on some tablets. It took a while before I noticed any effect, but talking helped. Eventually, I heard from a surgery who wanted to take on a willing trainee. The pay was awful, but it was what I wanted to do. My parents had one last go at trying to persuade me to go to university in September, but I wanted to follow my heart.

It was the best thing I ever did. I love what I do. I'm happy. I'm slowly coming off my tablets with my doctor's help and my parents are speaking to me. I still feel that my Dad's not that happy with me and resents my choice and that upsets me sometimes.

I just wish they'd understand.

(Name changed)

5

OTHER TYPES OF DEPRESSION

As you can see there are many different types and causes of depression and not all of them have the same symptoms. In this chapter, I will go into some of the other different types of depression which may affect people, whether reactive or endogenous.

Remember, that just because there are different types, it does not mean that a patient is restricted to just one kind of depression. A patient may have clinical depression and then suffer with an episode of post traumatic stress disorder. Another may have post-natal depression, but also suffer with seasonal affective disorder.

Read the differences below and see which of these you, or someone known to you, may relate to.

SEASONAL AFFECTIVE DISORDER (SAD)

SAD is a disorder which occurs in a patient according to the season of the year, typically as winter approaches. The patient's mood is drastically affected. Depression sets in and they feel sluggish, not only in body but also in the mind. Thought processes may be slow. They may be forgetful or irritated by small upsets. A lot of sufferers with SAD note a preponderance of needing lots of extra sleep, and general lethargy and malaise become quite a problem.

Other sufferers may note that their appetite does not so much increase (in that they feel hungry) but just that tend to eat more, especially carbohydrates and sugar rich foods, such as biscuits, cakes, potatoes. Low mood seems to be worse in the afternoons and evenings, but their symptoms start to resolve with the coming of spring time. (SAD may account for the higher suicide rates that occur during the winter months.)

Women seem to be affected by SAD more than men are, but what is SAD?

Some doctors believe that mood is related to light, as light is instrumental in the release of melatonin, a hormone created in the pineal gland. (Melatonin is a hormone that is released in the body when it is dark and not when the light is bright. Melatonin receptors in the brain react to the hormone and help the body to recognise when it is night-time and when it is day time.

Melatonin is derived from serotonin which helps work to regulate and organise a person's sleep patterns.)

If you are diagnosed with SAD (and please make sure that this is the condition you have, by seeing your GP) then you may find that you benefit from using Light Therapy. A lot of sufferers have found this type of therapy most effective and though they do not lose all of their depressive symptoms, they do feel a lot better in coping with their day and have more energy and 'get-up-and-go'.

Treatment consists of seating yourself in front of what is called a 'light box'. This is a box that contains full spectrum light and to feel any benefit, you have to sit in front of it for a few hours each day. This full spectrum light is a doppelganger of natural sunlight, the lack of which appears to be the cause of

SAD. Some sufferers state that they get the most benefit from this treatment if they use it in the mornings and results are usually seen after a week.

It is possible to buy your own light for use in the home, though it is best to buy one from a registered supplier, such as the SAD Association. The association may even be able to arrange for you to hire one from them for a lesser charge.

SAD Association
PO Box 989
Steyning
BN44 3HG
www.sada.org.uk

POST TRAUMATIC STRESS DISORDER

Post traumatic stress disorder is a difficult disorder to diagnose as the effects may not be seen immediately after an event.

PTSD is a reactive depression initially, which may then become endogenous. This condition occurs specifically after someone has been exposed to an extreme of stress such as a violent crime, being raped, witnessing a terrorist attack or being involved in one, serving during a war, etc.

The initial trauma of such a condition, may be experienced as flashbacks. The sufferer sees the event happening again, over and over in explicit detail, with sound, smell and sensory overdrive. The flashbacks can occur during the day, causing panic attacks, hyperventilation and nausea, or at night time when the patient is asleep, resulting in nightmares and broken sleep, sweating and feverishness.

The patient may stop eating, may stop venturing out and

withdraw from society, family and friends. They may become extremely irritable and snappy or even turn to a substance such as alcohol to cope with getting through the hours. At its worst extremes, a sufferer may even harbour thoughts of suicide, especially if they suffer feelings of 'survivor guilt'.

A GP will be able to diagnose the condition and it is one that will settle with time, but a patient usually requires external help with the support of skilled and registered counsellors, psychologists or psychiatrists, that may utilise Cognitive Behavioural Therapy (CBT) or Behaviour Therapy (BT).

BRAIN DAMAGE

Damage can occur to the brain through various ways, especially as a result of trauma/accident or disease and after damage has occurred, symptoms similar to depression may occur. (Hearing a diagnosis of brain damage can also be such a shock, it can be quite similar to the effect of PTSD.)

For example, Alzheimer's Disease (a form of dementia, characterised by short-term memory loss, deterioration in 'normal' behaviour and intellect) can be hidden by a previous diagnosis of depression, or even misdiagnosed as depression, especially in elderly patients.

Coping with a long-term illness or knowing you have a condition that is causing significant or insignificant brain damage can also cause the onset of depression.

Patients with a long-term illness or those that have suffered brain damage as the result of an accident, may be offered counselling to help cope with their condition in an attempt to help prevent the onset of depression. However, some patients may be so angry or in such denial that they refuse such offers. In these cases, it may be up to the family and friends of the patient to get the names and numbers of any helpful associations so that if the patient changes their mind at a later date and feels the need to just talk about how they feel, then they have somewhere and someone to whom they can go. (Of course, anyone can also see their own GP at any point.)

HAVING A DEPRESSIVE PERSONALITY

Having a depressing/pessimistic personality does not preclude someone from actually developing depression.

Depressive personality in itself in not an illness. It is a character trait. That person would be of the 'wine glass always being half-empty' kind of mindset. Normal everyday activities always have a down side. For example, any possible car journeys will be marred by their constant gloomy observations. Other drivers' bad habits, the amount of traffic, the fact that when they get to wherever they are going the place will no doubt be overrun and busy. They'll get upset at traffic lights and cyclists and generally everything is usually everyone else's fault or you hear 'this sort of thing always happens to me!'

Yet depressive personalities can also develop any kind of depression (my father has a pessimistic personality and also SAD) and it would take an extremely talented member of their family to notice if that person also suffered with depression.

ANXIETY DISORDER

If you have an anxiety disorder, it does not mean that you will automatically get a depressive disorder, but it can predispose you to it. Anxiety disorders may develop from phobias, psychosomatic illness (believeing there to be something wrong

49

with their body, when there isn't), obsessions and compulsions or a dysfunction in the body. Suffering with extreme nerves, not being confident or having good self-esteem can also create an anxiety disorder.

It is when these anxieties become so much part of the sufferers' life that it overtakes everything else that depression can set in. The event causing the anxiety controls so much of the sufferers' life that they feel they cannot do everyday things can lead to that depression and then the symptoms of depression also make everything a whole lot worse. It very much becomes a vicious cycle and can quite quickly become such an issue, the sufferer does not know what actually came first and what the root of their problem is!

Anxiety disorders can benefit greatly from cognitive behavioural therapy and general counselling and many people benefit from these types of treatment for their anxiety and depression.

6

TREATING DEPRESSION

You may suspect you have depression all by yourself and try to treat it on your own and this may or may not be successful. By and large, the most beneficial thing to do if you even suspect depression in any of its forms, is to go to your own doctor and have them diagnose it officially. Doctors do know what they are looking for and they are trained to spot it and they also have all the contact details of people who may be able to help you.

If you feel you just cannot see your own doctor for whatever reason and that you are feeling really low, you can contact the Samaritans or walk into your local hospital's A&E, especially if you feel that you may harm yourself and there you will be assessed by an on call psychiatrist or a member of their crisis prevention team. These people are there for a reason and will listen to you, so do not worry that they may think your worries and problems are trivial or silly.

They will not.

Professionals have various ways of treating depression according to the age of the patient and what kind of depression they are suffering from and we will look at each of these closely so you may know what to expect if you are referred for any of them. In any case, there is never any reason to be afraid of your treatment for depression.

It is there to help get you better and each professional will help you get better at your own pace. If you do not feel ready to try something, then you will be allowed to say so. If there is something you are not ready to talk about, then they will go around the issue until you feel ready to delve into it.

Ultimately, they are there to help you.

So what can you expect if you decide to go to your GP?

First of all, your doctor will discuss with you what you think your overall problem is and then they will check you over to make sure you are not suffering with a physical illness. This may or may not include a blood test. Your doctor may offer you medication, or refer you to a counsellor, especially if your depression is only mild. However, you may feel that you do not want medication or do not want to talk to someone and in this case, if you do not get better on your own, you can always come back again to your GP.

If your depression is severe, your doctor may strongly recommend you take the tablets he/she has prescribed and refer you to a psychiatrist. Your GP may also want you to come back after a few weeks for a check-up to see how you are getting on with your tablets and whether the dosage or variant of medication needs alteration.

After a few weeks on medication, you should of course, start to notice some benefits. Most patients report that they notice their sleep patterns and appetite improve first before any effect is felt on the actual depression, but you may be different. You may feel that you no longer want to take your tablets, but never stop taking anti-depressants without consulting your doctor as you may need to be 'weaned' off them slowly to prevent any adverse side-effects.

If tablets do not work and you are still severely depressed you may be offered hospital treatment, possibly admitted if the situation is extremely bad and you are suicidal.

However, different doctors may proceed differently, depending upon the case.

PSYCHOLOGICAL THERAPY

Psychology deals with the study of behaviour and all of its related mental processes. It mainly concerns itself with rational and irrational thoughts, memories, learning, personality, emotions and their relationship to behaviour.

There are different schools of psychological thought, such as those that believe in Freud, or Jung. But there are also those that believe in behaviourism and cognition as being more important and leading the way, and certainly, cognitive behavioural therapy, at the moment, seems to be 'all the rage'. yet having said this, it does not mean that all psychologists belong to one school of thought or another. There are many professionals who take a little from each of the beliefs and apply it to their individual clients according to the problems being presented, as different therapies benefit different conditions and different clients.

Psychological therapy will best suit those patients who do not want to take any medication for their depression. Also, there are some clients who really benefit from getting deep into their mental and emotional past to find the root causes for their depression, because in the present, they just cannot see a reason for their condition.

Therapy however, takes time and commitment from the patient to keep going. This isn't just a one-off session you will have. You may have to go to the counsellor/psychologist many times and make the trip in your car, on the bus or train. And as we know, if you are depressed, you may not feel like going anywhere. You can be exhausted and lethargic. Perhaps you need time or even medication to make you feel a little better before you see a psychologist?

Each therapy session usually consists of one hour, once a week, but can be for longer or even more frequently depending upon how you are in yourself or how severe your problem is.

COGNITIVE BEHAVIOURAL THERAPY (CBT)

Cognitive Behavioural Therapy is a type of psychotherapy which is based on the belief that psychological problems are there because of a patients' faulty way of thinking about their world. The cognitive behavioural therapist listens to, assists and helps that patient identify these faulty ways of thinking and shows them a different way of thinking to avoid the initial problem.

Cognitive Behavioural Therapy is an excellent therapy to use in the cases of a depressed person. After your initial session, you may be asked to record any and all negative thoughts that you may have about anything. You may then be asked to write about why you think in that way. The therapist, at later sessions will then go with you through your list and help you challenge those thoughts, especially any that are illogical or unrealistic and may show you alternative ways to tackle a certain individual thought. You may be set homework after each session (but don't think of this as homework you used to get at school where you had to write three pages of

A4!). This homework could be for you to challenge another thought on your own or think about what was discussed that day and practice it at home; letting your therapist know at the next session how it went and whether you feel any of it has been successful.

CBT seems to work well in mild, moderate, or even severe, depressive cases, and remember, it can also be used in conjunction with medication, or without. It can be down to your choice, but always discuss the pros and cons of taking/not taking medication with your GP, especially if your depression is moderate to severe.

BEHAVIOUR THERAPY

Behaviour therapy is completely different to cognitive therapy in that cognitive therapy tackles how you think, whereas behaviour therapy tackles what you do. It does not focus on why you feel so depressed, but rather acts on making you act less depressed. For example, you would be encouraged and educated in how to look after yourself better. A superior eating programme and lifestyle, ensuring your sleep patterns are regular and making sure you get a good amount of exercise, the theory being that if you look after yourself better, behave better, it stops you slumping into the depression as you are actively taking care of yourself.

This kind of therapy may benefit those with less severe cases of depression and those people who always feel better doing something about problems, rather than talking about them.Remember, not everyone is comfortable talking about their problems or how they think or what happened in their past. They may do eventually, but to start off with, behavioural therapy could help because the patient is physically involved in tackling their problem.

PSYCHOANALYSIS

This is a long-term treatment, developing over many sessions and many topics, not just the depression, but also other events in your life.

Psychoanalysts believe that any problems we have in our current lives, and the problems they are causing, have their origins in our pasts. That these past problems were something we did not deal with at the time and so now they are 'rearing their heads' in our current lives. These past problems may have been ignored or denied. Or we may have even tried to forget them, believing that if we don't think about them, giving them their power, then they will go away, only to have these problems haunt us in the present. Festering away in the backs of our minds and causing us upset and possibly the depression that sent us to them in the first place.

These past events do not always have to be intensely tragic. They can be somewhat vague too, but as time accumulates, these problems build up in our minds and strike us down when we are weak or under stress, because we just didn't deal with them at the time they occurred.

Psychoanalysis is said to work by the way it assists these past, darker feelings in coming to the forefront of our minds, allowing us to see them for what they are. Analyse them. Talk about them. Deal with them. In effect, lessening the effect the past pain used to have and weakening its effect, allowing you, as a whole person, to move on. It allows repressed thoughts to the surface and encourages 'free-thinking'.

Your GP can refer you to a professional psychoanalyst, but if you choose to do so yourself, then make sure you go to a practitioner who is registered with an official body as anyone can call themselves a counsellor and you do not wish to have your life rummaged through by someone who is poorly trained or ill educated about matters of the mind.

COUNSELLING

Counsellors do exactly as they are described. They counsel. They help you to solve a problem, maybe suggesting another way you could tackle certain issues and encourage you to think about things and life. They will not give specific advice but will assist you in helping to sort your problems.

A counsellor will be sympathetic and listen carefully, allowing you to do most of the talking. They will clarify your problems for you if you have difficulties seeing them for what they are.

Again, anyone can call themselves a counsellor, so ask your GP to recommend you to someone. (Some GP practices retain the services of their own surgery counsellor.)

WHAT CAN YOU EXPECT FROM COUNSELLING AND PSYCHOTHERAPY?

These are services designed to help people who wish to make changes in their lives by offering 'talking treatment'. However, specific advice is not given.

HOW COULD A THERAPIST HELP ME?

You should expect one or a series of confidential, professional appointments of up to an hour in length in a suitable private setting.

WHAT ARE THE KEY ELEMENTS OF THIS PROCESS?
- Service provided when you wish to make changes in your life
- An opportunity to make sense of your individual circumstances ·
- Contact with a therapist who helps identify the choices for change ·
- Support for the individual during their process of change ·

The end result leaving you better equipped to cope for the future.

DO I HAVE TO LIE ON A COUCH?
There are many different, valid ways of undertaking therapy. In most cases, though not always, you would be offered a chair to sit on.

HOW DO THERAPISTS WORK, THEN?
They usually work face-to-face employing a range of techniques to suit your circumstances. However, with the advent of the Internet some therapists may use a mixture of telephone, email and video conferencing.

WHY ARE THERE DIFFERENT APPROACHES?
Different therapies have different styles. For instance, in cognitive behavioural and sex therapy there will be 'homework'

to do. In bereavement therapy, there would be a lot of emphasis on supporting you through some difficult emotions. A psychodynamic counsellor would look at your past while another type of therapist might focus solely on your life in the present-day. Some therapies concentrate on the future.

HOW DO THEY WORK?

Many approaches regard your developing relationship with the therapist as a kind of model which may reveal the patterns of behaviour that cause you problems. Others look at your family relationships and who wielded the power in your house when you were growing up. Others focus on your thinking style and changes in behaviour. There are big distinctions between therapy where you do most of the talking and those which involve much more of a dialogue. But don't worry, whichever approach is adopted you should be able to make the changes you are looking for. The first appointment, sometimes called an assessment session, is an opportunity to explore issues that could affect the relationship between you and the counsellor/psychotherapist as well as your personal needs for counselling

WILL I GET HOOKED ON THERAPY?

The goal of any talking treatment is your increased self-awareness, skill acquisition and independence. During therapy, you may develop some feelings of reliance upon the therapist. Although a normal reaction it can, at times, feel worrying. But a professional therapist knows exactly how to handle these feelings and is genuinely interested in helping you make progress.

IS THERE A COUNSELLOR OR THERAPIST FOR MY SITUATION?

Therapists practise in all walks of life and all parts of society - from an NHS clinic to the Boardrooms of top companies. We are trained in situations as diverse as: coping with anxiety and bereavement, relationship difficulties, educational dilemmas, sexual and racial issues, personal problem-solving as well as helping victims of child abuse and trauma.

WHERE CAN I FIND A THERAPIST?

You can use BACP and its directories to find a therapist. Always enquire whether a potential therapist is bound by BACP's ethical guidelines and professional conduct.

WHAT IF I AM DEAF OR HEARING IMPAIRED?

You can contact BACP via its minicom service on 0870 4435162 for assistance in trying to locate accessible practitioners or services.

WHAT SHOULD I ASK WHEN I CONTACT A COUNSELLOR OR PSYCHOTHERAPIST FOR THE FIRST TIME?

Ask about the time, place, cost and duration of meetings plus any charges for cancelled appointments and holidays. You may also wish to enquire about the counsellor or psychotherapist's professional membership, experience and training. During this time you will build up an idea of what is involved and you will be able to make up your mind if this is a person you can work with. It is important to be clear about what you want and what the practitioner is able to offer.

IS COUNSELLING AND PSYCHOTHERAPY CONFIDENTIAL?

Everything you discuss is confidential between you and the counsellor or psychotherapist. There can be certain legal exceptions and the practitioner should clarify this with you prior to the establishment of any agreed contract for working.

WHAT IS SUPERVISION?

All BACP therapists need to be in supervision which is a form of consultative support and must therefore discuss their work with at least one other person. But a supervisor is also bound by rules of confidentiality so in practice there is no likelihood of any breach of trust.

HOW MUCH WILL IT COST?

Costs can vary widely - fees are usually higher in the big population centres - so it is important to establish how much you will be paying before entering a mutual contractual arrangement. You could expect to pay anything between £10 and £80+ per session.

WHAT IF I AM ON A LOW INCOME OR UNEMPLOYED?

If you are on a limited budget then fees can sometimes be adjusted to meet your situation and your ability to pay.

WHAT IF I AM A STUDENT?

Students can seek counselling/psychotherapy from staff employed by their training institute, university or college and special or no-fee arrangements may apply. Always check beforehand.

WHAT IF I AM NOT HAPPY WITH THE COUNSELLOR OR PSYCHOTHERAPIST WHEN WE MEET?

During the Assessment or first session, be prepared to trust your instinct because your relationship with the therapist is at the heart of the work. If you are unsure about the practitioner seek another one. Having confidence in your practitioner is very important and will enable you to get the best out of the time you spend together. Always remember it is you who are the customer.

WHAT ABOUT COUNSELLING OR PSYCHOTHERAPY ONLINE?

There are a number of counsellors now offering an online service. Before entering into any contractual arrangement you should satisfy yourself that the practitioner is qualified to provide the service and is a member of a professional body like BACP. Although in some situations there are benefits to counselling through the Internet, confidentiality is a key concern. For example, you may wish to ask if your notes are protected by passwords and encrypted? Are printouts held in a secure cabinet? What happens when there are technical problems or the practitioner is away?

Remember that online discussions must pass through an Internet Service Provider (ISP) where security may not be a high priority.

HOW CAN I BE SURE A COUNSELLOR OR PSYCHOTHERAPIST IS QUALIFIED?

Ask us. BACP is the largest voice of the talking therapies in the UK. BACP members are covered by an Ethical Framework for Good Practice in Counselling and Psychotherapy and a Professional Conduct Procedure.

We at BACP can refer you to:

- Accredited counsellors registered with the British Association for Counselling and Psychotherapy (BACP)
- the UK Register of Counsellors (UKRC)
- the UK Council for Psychotherapists Register of Psychotherapists (UKCP)
- the British Psychoanalytic Council (BPC)
- the British Psychological Society Register of Chartered Psychologists (BPS)
- COSCA (Counselling and Psychotherapy in Scotland) accredited members
- practising members of the British Association for Counselling and Psychotherapy who are properly supervised.

HOW CAN I FIND A COUNSELLOR OR PSYCHOTHERAPIST WHO SPEAKS MY LANGUAGE?

Some practitioners are multi-lingual. In the BACP Directory these languages are listed. If you would prefer to communicate in language other than English then ask the practitioner or check with BACP.

WILL A COUNSELLOR OR PSYCHOTHERAPIST SEE ME STRAIGHT AWAY?

Every effort will be made to see you at a time to suit. Sometimes demand for individuals or in organisations for counselling/psychotherapy can mean waiting lists.

How can I get counselling/psychotherapy for a member of my family or a friend?

You cannot. A person cannot be 'sent' for counselling or psychotherapy. They must wish to use the service and make the approach themselves. By all means, find out the names of therapists on their behalf but please encourage a direct approach by the person who needs the help.

WHERE CAN I FIND OUT MORE?

COSCA (Counselling and Psychotherapy in Scotland) |
www.cosca.org.uk
18 Viewfield Street, STIRLING, FK8 1UA
Tel: 01786 475140

UK Register of Counsellors | www.ukrconline.org.uk
PO Box 1050, RUGBY, Warwickshire CV21 2HZ
Tel: 01788 568739

Irish Association for Counselling | www.irish-counselling.ie
8 Cumberland Street, Dun Laoghaire, County Dublin
Tel: 00 353 1 230 0061

Alcohol Concern | www.alcoholconcern.org.uk
Waterbridge House, 32-36 Loman Street, LONDON, SE1 0EE
Tel: 020 7928 7377

Mind - The Mental Health Charity | www.mind.org.uk
15-19 Broadway, LONDON, E15 4BQ
Tel: 020 8519 2122

Nafsiyat Inter-Cultural Therapy Centre | www.nafsiyat.org.uk
278 Seven Sisters Road, Finsbury Park, LONDON, N4 2HY
Tel: 020 7263 4130

Relate | www.relate.org.uk
Herbert Gray College, Little Church Street, RUGBY, CV21 3AP
Tel: 01788 573241

(The above information about what to expect from counselling or psychotherapy was kindly reprinted with permission from the British Association of Counsellors and Psychotherapists and is also available on their website.)

ANTIDEPRESSANTS
Antidepressant medication is very effective in treating depression, but a lot of people are afraid to take it, for fear of becoming dependent on the drugs, or worrying that the medication will somehow change who they are.

However, if antidepressants are taken the correct way, as prescribed, you should notice a good start to your improvement in mood within the first month, if not the first couple of weeks. Thereafter, you should take them for at least six months after the depression has lifted and then discuss with your GP the correct way to come off the tablets, without suffering any adverse side effects or problems. You cannot become addicted to antidepressants. You will not develop a 'high' when you take a tablet and then suffer a 'downer' when you're ready for another dose. Antidepressants only work if you suffer with depression.

If you do not have depression and you take an antidepressant you will notice nothing. Yet do not misunderstand. Antidepressants are powerful drugs, filled with strong medication and if you stop taking them suddenly, without coming off them carefully, you may feel quite out-of-sorts. This does not mean that you have become addicted to your antidepressants. It just means that your system has become accustomed to having the presence of them in your body. They are providing something that should be there in the first place and if you come off them when you are not ready, then you will suffer side-effects. Removing them from your system gradually, under medical supervision, will ensure there are no symptoms and if you do suffer a reaction of any kind, then your doctor will be on hand to advise you.

HOW DO ANTIDEPRESSANTS HELP?

If you have read the earlier chapters, then you will thoroughly understand the simple fact that if you are depressed, then there are physical changes inside your body, making it work and react in a different way to 'normal'. Also, I went into some small detail about nerves, synapses and neurotransmitters in the brain. (For those of you who need a quick recap, the human brain requires there to be enough neurotransmitter in the synaptic space between nerve cells to pass messages on from one part of the brain to another.) Neurotransmitters that are released by the brain are used or reabsorbed back into the cell from which they came.

If you suffer with depression, no matter which kind, then your level of neurotransmitters is low. For your brain to return to its optimum and for your mental health to be fully restored, this level has to be raised once again and this, basically, is how antidepressants work. However, different drugs and medications work in differing ways and affect different parts of the brain's make-up.

For example, some drugs will prevent any released neurotransmitters that are in the synaptic space from being reabsorbed back into the cells, therefore leaving a person with a normal level of neurotransmitter. These drugs are known as tricyclics or serotonin specific re-uptake inhibitors (or SSRIs, for short).

TRICYCLICS

Tricyclics are so called because they have a basic chemical structure of three benzene rings. The most commonly prescribed of these are: amitriptyline (trade names of Elavil or Lentizol); doxepin (trade names of Xepin or Sinequan) and imipramine (trade name - Tofranil). Obviously all medicines come with information sheets and you must discuss the side effects with your doctor if they concern or bother you. Make sure you are not allergic to any of the ingredients before taking and if you have Coeliac's Disease as well (an intolerance to gluten), remember to check which kind of starch is contained within the tablet.

Tricyclic medication works best when the depression is moderate to severe and the patient suffers with sleep problems and appetite disturbances. Once a patient begins taking them, it can take up to two weeks before any beneficial effect is noted. However, your doctor will want to take into account your symptoms from your depression as tricyclics also come in three other separate categories: sedative; non-sedative and stimulants. Depending upon how your depression affects your mood, will direct your doctor in the direction of the correct medication to suit you. If you already feel lethargic and feel that your every movement is like wading through glue, then a non-sedative tricyclic such as Imipramine (Tofranil) may be prescribed. If your depression makes you irritable and on-edge, then your GP may prescribe a sedative tricyclic to help calm you, such as Amitriptyline (Elavil, Lentizol).

Any side-effects that are bothersome for you can be reduced or gotten rid of by discussing with your doctor the fact that you might need to start again on a low level dose of your medication and then slowly building the level up (with your GP's supervision) as your body copes with the changes.

Be aware that tricyclics can affect other medications, so double check that you can have your tricyclics with your doctor and only take what the doctor has prescribed. Overdosing on tricyclics can possibly be fatal, so if there is anyone in your home who may be suicidal, these tricyclics must be locked away or kept in small amounts so that an overdose is not physically possibly.

SEROTONIN SPECIFIC RE-UPTAKE INHIBITORS (SSRIs)

SSRIs work quite similarly to tricyclics, except that they only work on the one kind of neurotransmitter.

They are quite popular as they appear to have less side-effects than the tricyclics and have a lower sedative quality. (Epileptics must take these with caution, however as they can cause stomach problems such as nausea, vomiting and diarrhoea.) Yet, some doctors will only prescribe SSRIs if they feel the patient is unable to take tricyclic medication.

One SSRI that is quite well known by most people - even those without depression or mental health problems - is fluoxetine, or to give it its more common name, Prozac. It has received much press and is known as a 'happy pill' because of its ability to make mildly depressed people return to how they were before they had depression. With less side effects than a tricyclic, it was also easier for some people to take, though some GPs worried that it was being overprescribed and that a lot of people receiving Prozac, didn't really need it, and as their depression was only mild in the first place, would probably have got better on their own anyway. It is a debatable point.

Other SSRIs are: citalopram (trade name Cipramil); sertraline (trade name Lustral); fluvoxamine (trade name Faverin) and paroxetine (trade name Seroxat).

MONOAMINE OXIDASE INHIBITORS (MAOIs)

Monoamine oxidase is an enzyme an enzymes work as catalysts. This particular one oxidates monamines (serotonin, adrenaline and noradrenaline). MAOIs inhibit this enzyme and therefore it is used in the treatment of depression.

MAOIs were, in fact, the first antidepressants produced for the treatment of depression and so they have a longer history than any other medication.

If we go back to those synapses and neurotransmitters we remember that the cells release the neurotransmitter and if not used they are broken up and reabsorbed by the cell that produced it. The MAOI stops the monoamine oxidase breaking the neurotransmitter down, leaving the neurotransmitter level at the required level.

However, this enzyme, monoamine oxidase, is also present elsewhere in the body, specifically the liver, where it works to break down another chemical called tyramine. Tyramine is found in cheese and too high a level of it in the body can cause health problems such as high blood pressure, headache and eventually, stroke. Therefore anyone taking MAOIs must restrict themselves to a low tyramine food programme.

When you finish taking a course of MAOIs, it will take up to two weeks for your body to produce new monoamine oxidase, so you must stick to the diet for this time. Also, if the MAOIs had no effect on your depression, then during that two week period you will be unable to take any other antidepressant.

Because of this problem, scientists have come up with a different MAOI called a reversible inhibitor of monoamine oxidase or RIMA. RIMAs block the action of monoamine oxydase. They do not destroy it like the MAOIs. Therefore a person's body does not have to make new monoamine oxydase, the effects are 'reversible' and have completely worn off twenty four hourse after stopping taking the drug.

Some known MAOIs are: phenelzine (trade name Nardil); moclobemide (RIMA. Trade name Manerix); isocarboxazid and tranylcypromine (trade name Parnate).

OTHERS

Flupentixol (trade names are Depixol and Fluanxol) is a strong drug used for patients whose depression has also made them suffer with psychoses or schizophrenia. It works by prolonging the action of serotonin in the brain, rather like an SSRI and works well in low doses for depression. It is not fatal if taken as an overdose and does not appear to have many side effects, though there are serious side effects if this drug is taken for a long time. Therefore GPs only use this as a short term medication.

LITHIUM

This is an oral drug, given to patients suffering from severe depression or those who have suffered repeat bouts of depression or episodes of psychosis. It is also a very effective drug in treating bi-polar disorder or manic depression.

Lithium is very similar to sodium (salt) and therefore some people taking this drug may experience side effects such as excessive thirst or urination. However, as with other medications, some patients may not experience any side effects at all. It all comes down to the individual.

This particular drug has to be taken regularly and the level in the blood has to be checked. If a person does not take enough lithium then it will not have any effect on that person. Yet too much lithium can cause a person to suffer a lot of side effects, such as those described above as well as tremors, weakness and nausea. In extreme cases, it can be life threatening.

Each patient taking lithium for depression, will undergo blood tests to check the right level for them. You will even be asked to provide blood samples before starting on lithium to ensure that your kidneys are working correctly and efficiently and that all the other chemicals in your blood are at the right levels. You may receive a general physical examination and a heart trace may be taken to also check that your heart has no problems before starting lithium treatment.

The thyroid gland can be affected by taking this drug, so this will also be checked. (The thyroid gland is important to maintain your metabolic rate.) If you show any signs of having any irregularities with your kidneys, heart or thyroid, then you will be unable to take lithium to treat your depression.

However, if your blood tests come back clear and you are started on a course of lithium, you will usually have weekly blood tests to check the lithium level until your body gets accustomed to the dosage prescribed, and then if everything is going normally, those blood tests will only be required monthly for about three months. After this point in time, your own GP will decide how often they require you to have a blood test.

When on lithium, you have to be very aware of what is happening to your body and normal things that you wouldn't really worry about, should be considered to have an affect on your lithium levels.

For example, if you were to contract a sickness or diarrhoea bug and you were losing a lot of fluid, then you would have to see your doctor to have another blood test. The same would apply if you were to go travelling in a very hot country where there would be a strong possibility of becoming dehydrated from overly hot weather. You would also have to consider whether you would be allowed to take water tablets whilst on lithium. But all of these points would have to be discussed with your own GP.

Experiencing any side effects of lithium may be uncomfortable to start, but they may also be mild, or even non-existent. However, if they do exist, take comfort in the fact that they usually pass with time. The general side effects of shaking hands, tremors, nausea, metallic taste in the mouth and/or a dry mouth are normal, but if they become extremely severe (say you get incredibly weak, you're feeling really sick, are vomiting or getting confused) then you must see your doctor immediately, or even go to an A&E department and let them know that you are on lithium treatment.

These extreme signs can be evidence that your body is suffering from too much of the drug and your system is unable to cope with it.

You may experience some mild weight gain whilst on lithium, so be extra sure to watch your diet and eat healthily, taking in the recommended amount of fruit and vegetables each day and drinking the correct amount of water for you.

If you suspect that you are pregnant whilst you are taking lithium then see your doctor immediately as it is not advised to be on lithium whilst in the early stages of pregnancy. Therefore, if you are considering starting a family (or even if your depression is caused by a failure to conceive, yet you are still trying) then you should let your doctor know when you go to see them, so that they do not prescribe this particular medication.

Once the placenta has become established, three or four months into the pregnancy, then lithium may be taken and your levels will be monitored closely.

MOOD STABILISERS
Some doctors may prefer to try you out on a mood stabiliser, more commonly given to epileptic patients, if you are unsuitable to take lithium. These anticonvulsant drugs are used in people who have seizures but do not show themselves as having convulsions. They are called carbamazepine (trade name Tegretol. Can actually be used with lithium), lamotrigine (trade name Lamictal), phenytoin (trade name Epanutin), sodium valproate (trade name Epilim. To be used with caution in pregnancy), topiramate, gabapentin, levetiracetam, oxcarbazepine and vigabatrin.

COMING OFF THE MEDICATION
Let us imagine for a minute that you have been successfully taking an anti-depressant for your condition and you are now wanting to come off the drug. Or at least, your doctor has suggested you begin to think about doing so.

How do you do it?

Well, the simple answer, is to do this under medical supervision. Otherwise, there can be a variety of problems.

Case study
Melanie*, 68

I'd been taking amitriptyline for many many years, ever since I'd had my last child. I was sick of taking tablets. Every day I had to do it and I thought to myself, "well, I seem okay now".

I was determined to cut down the amount I was taking. I had been taking two tablets a day. One in the morning and one at night and so I thought that if I cut it down gradually, then I'd be okay. I knew better than to go cold turkey. I wasn't idiotic. I began by cutting my evening tablet in half every other day and did this for a few weeks. I didn't notice any side effects, so I started to cut my morning tablet in half too. After a week, I thought I was doing well and had booked an appointment at my doctors to let him know what I was doing.

However, two nights before I was due to see him, I got up during the night to use the loo and felt all dizzy and sick. I actually collapsed in the bathroom and hit my head on the sink as I went down. Apparently I passed out. My husband found me and called the emergency doctors out. They were very good to me. I hadn't hurt my head badly and I didn't have to go into hospital. But for those next two days I felt awful! My head was woolly-feeling and I didn't feel like I was in my own body. It was like it was someone else talking. Someone else doing things and I was just an eye witness or something.

My doctor was not happy with me for cutting the drug down so quickly and so drastically on my own. He made me get back on my usual dosage and said that when I'd fully recovered, he would help me try and wean myself off properly when I felt ready to try again. Only I don't feel ready. I feel off a lot of the time and my head just isn't right. And to be honest, I don't think I'm brave enough to come off them again. I guess I'll be on them for a lot longer and really, what trouble is it jsyt to swallow a couple of tablets a day?

'Melanie' learnt the hard way. Even though she thought she was reducing her medication gradually, she wasn't doing it gradually enough and experienced a frightening episode that has now affected the way she thinks about her medication.

The important things to always remember when wanting to come off your anti-depressants are:

- Always discuss it with your GP or consultant first
- You cannot stop taking them cold turkey. A patient must be weaned off gradually under medical supervision
- By following your doctor's advice, you can avoid many possible withdrawal symptoms (light-headedness, dizzy spells, nausea, vomiting, loss of appetite, headache, sleep disturbances, anxiety and restlessness)

7

SELF-HARMING AND SUICIDE

Unfortunately, some people suffering with depression, will feel the need to self-harm or harbour thoughts of committing suicide. The two are not inexorably linked. If you self-harm, it does not necessarily mean you will think of, or try to commit suicide. And if you feel suicidal, it does not mean that you will have previously self-harmed. Only sometimes a few people will harm themselves before going on to think or try to kill themselves.

Self-harming can take many forms. Sufferers may poison themselves with a deliberate overdose of some harmful substance (but not enough to be fatal) to suffer the consequences. They may hit themselves where bruises will not be seen or where an explanation can be readily created. (eg, "Oh, I caught my leg on the corner of the table.") Others may cut themselves with blades or broken glass, they might attempt to burn themselves with lit cigarettes or hold their hands over a lighted match. Some will pull at their hair, often removing huge amounts or pick at their skin, peeling it away until it bleeds. Others may scratch themselves or pinch themselves, whilst others may attempt more brutal forms such as self-strangulation until the feeling of passing out comes close, before they stop.

But why do people self-harm? What do they get from it, when they know it is wrong and that presumably, it is going to cause them pain?

Case study
Tracey*, 38

I suffered from a terrible phobia as a child. I was scared of busy places. Places where there seemed to be hundreds of people bustling about, so going to school was terrifying for me. I'd tried to tell my parents how I'd felt, but like any parents, they put it down to me being nervous of going to big school. They really thought it was something I'd either grow out of, or lose when I began to make friends. Only I didn't. My fear got worse. I began to get what I now know was claustrophobia, but at the time, I didn't have the words to explain what I was feeling.

To stop going to school, I used to pretend I felt sick, and when that stopped working, I'd sit in my bedroom at the weekends and bash away at my foot with the wooden edge of an old tennis racket, hoping to break the bones. I thought, that if I couldn't walk, then I wouldn't get sent to school. I never realised that I'd be given crutches, I wasn't thinking that far ahead. Only I never broke the bones. It hurt too much. I just got left with some bruising, which didn't earn much sympathy from my parents. After that, I started sticking myself with my mothers' old sewing needles, trying to rip the skin open. Seeing the blood was like being released of all the pain inside. Watching it trickle across my skin made me feel alive and in control for the first time. Until my brother caught me doing it. He told my parents and they told me off. My father locked me in my room which made me have this massive panic attack and soon I was bouncing off the walls, giving myself bruises I could never have dreamt of creating. I was taken to the doctor and given medication. They said I was suffering with nervous depression. The tablets made me better and I coped better with school, but the thoughts to harm were still there and I even once thought of suicide. I never did anything about it though.

Tracey, and a lot of other self-harmers will admit that the act of harming seems to relieve some of the pressure inside. Some refer to it as a 'silent scream'. Sufferers who harm themselves feel sad or lonely, they are usually unable to communicate their feelings effectively (like we saw in Tracey's story) or they consider themselves to be failures at what they do. Some sufferers may believe that no-one cares about them anyway, or they feel pretty hopeless about what the future might bring. Others may start to self harm because they suffer a string of upsets in a relatively short time or suffer a major relationship breakdown. Whatever the reason, people who self-harm say that apart from relieving the pain inside, it also makes them feel that over this act, of mutilation or whatever they choose to do to themselves, they feel that at last, they have some control.

There has been a huge increase in numbers of people who self-harm over the last few decades (source: Royal College of Psychiatrists), though whether that has more to do with current awareness or people feeling more able to admit they need help, than before, when mental illness was hidden and not talked about, cannot be proven.

Each year in the United Kingdom, hospitals see on average about 150,000 cases of people who have self-harmed deliberately, the most common method being a paracetemol overdose. (This particular method being extremely dangerous and in some cases, fatal. An overdose of paracetemol can cause serious liver damage, if it is not dealt with by medics.)

Self-harming in children is more often seen in girls than boys. It is always a sign that there is something wrong or disturbing going on with the child and they will always need to see a doctor if they are to be properly helped. It is not a source of attention-seeking, as some people believe and in children particularly, the act of harming themselves, definitely makes them feel like they have some control over what happens to them, in a world where adults and parents seem to call all of the shots. (One in ten young children who self-harm, will do so again on repeat occasions. Source: Mental Health Foundation, 2000)

HOW DO YOU STOP YOURSELF SELF-HARMING?
It would be nice to say that it can be stopped easily, and in a few cases, it probably has. But for the majority of sufferers, a lot of hard work goes into it. They receive medication, counselling, support. They need time.

Jack* 22
This must be what being an alcoholic is like. I used to self-harm and I haven't done so for a while now, but the thoughts are always there that I can do it, if I wanted to.

The 'temptation' to return to an old behaviour can be very strong, especially if someone has been self-harming themselves for a long time.

But self-harmers must feel positive when they even think of stopping. Because that is a huge step forward to them. To be able to realise that what they are doing is the wrong way to help themselves. So thinking about stopping is good.

However, along with those thoughts of stopping, some sufferers may recognise the worry about how else they might cope with pressures and life, if they are not going to self-harm.

- What if I continue to have all these bad feelings about myself?
- I still don't know why I do it in the first place. What if I can't stop?
- I can't control all these feelings
- I feel so bad about harming myself, but I need it
- People see my scars. They'll think I'm still doing it anyway
- I need people to understand. To listen when I talk
- People who know I self-harm think I'm mad anyway

Self-harming is not a realistic way to deal with stress and upset or depression. It just appears that way to the sufferer at the time. So what they need, are new ways of thinking and to be given new coping mechanisms, along with any medication prescribed by their doctor. Yet even if they do have medication and they do have a psychotherapist or counsellor to talk to, the self-harmer must realise that they are the ones who must ultimately help themselves. Others can listen. Others can support you and try to understand or give you advice. They can give you anti-depressants. But it must come from the inside of the sufferer. They are the ones that have to put the work in to make themselves better. To think and be positive. To deal with life's problems and issues as they come up, as they frequently do.

One of the first steps a self-harmer must consider, is why they self-harm in the first place? Many may not know the answer to this one. A few may think it obvious. But to those who don't know, this can be the most frightening thing. However, stopping themselves self-harming can only be an easy thing, if they find other ways of coping. Of knowing what their possible triggers are that make them self-harm.

They may like to think over the next few questions:

- How were you feeling when you first self-harmed?
- What was happening in your life at that time?
- What were your triggers to make you continue to self-harm?
- Where do you self-harm? Is it always the same place?
- Is there anything inside of you (thoughts, memories, etc) that are terrifying you that you haven't told anyone about?
- How do you feel after you have self-harmed?

Self-harmers really need to think about these points. Because if they can see some kind of recurring issue within their answers, then they will be one step closer to understanding why they self-harm and what they need to look out for the next time they get upset and feel the need to do it.

Next, they need to think of other ways in which they might cope. Most people when they get upset feel able to cope with it without hurting themselves. What do they do to get them through a difficult time in their lives? Personally, I know I can telephone my mother and discuss things through with her. Frequently she'll just listen and give a little advice or guidance without telling me what to do. But just knowing I have her there at the other end of the phone is a great comfort. But what else do I do? My mother won't always be around. Well, I put on the television and find a comedy to watch. Whose Line Is It Anyway? always makes me laugh, no matter how I'm feeling and if it's not on when I need it, I can watch clips on YouTube. Other times I'll go to the library and read. Or play with my children. Have a long soak in a bath full of bubbles. Listen to some upbeat music. Or eat a favourite bar of chocolate! Basically, reading through my own list, I can see that when I'm upset at something, I allow myself an indulgence. I treat myself to make myself feel better until my equilibrium returns.

What do you do? Think about it for a moment and see if there's a pattern.

GETTING HELP

Of course talking about (or reading about!) changing your ways, is easy. Doing it is the hard part and a self-harmer will not be able to get through this process alone. I'm sure there will be at least one previous self-harmer out there who will say that they did it on their own without help and that's great, but the majority, will need assistance.

Firstly, a self-harmer needs to find someone that they can trust implicitly. This person can be their doctor, or a long standing friend or a member of their family, perhaps even their counsellor, but it needs to be someone that they can tell all of their feelings to without worrying about being judged or admonished. And this part of the process is a huge step, because usually, those that self-harm do so in private. It is their own private way of dealing with how they feel with all their own issues and problems and suddenly they are going to have to share this with someone else. Their own anguish. Their pain. It won't be private anymore and just the thought of doing this can be scary.

(If you yourself are the self-harmer and you feel that there is no-one around you who you can trust like this, then maybe you ought to consider talking to someone over the phone. There are various helplines that can help and it might relax you more not having to talk face-to-face. And you have the added bonus of ending the conversation when you want. Details of helplines are listed at the back of this book.)

Choosing a professional such as your doctor, counsellor or therapist may be a good choice. They won't judge you, think you're mad or wasting time and everything you tell them is strictly confidential.

The important thing in this situation, is that once you have taken the decision to tell someone about what you are doing, then you must persist in finding someone who will listen to you. Don't ever give up, because you've managed to take a huge step in just wanting to share your problem.

'I KNOW SOMEONE WHO SELF-HARMS'

But what if you aren't the self-harmer, but you suspect that you know one?

First of all, you must make absolutely sure that the person is self-harming. Otherwise, you are going to find yourself in an extremely embarrassing or even volatile, situation. However, once you are sure that what you suspect is correct, then there are certain things you can do to help that person.

- Tell them you know and offer to listen to them.
- Offer your support
- Help them get the help they need, or go with them (if you can) to doctor's appointments. (Just sitting with them in the waiting room can provide a great comfort.)
- Do not judge them.
- Carry on doing normal everyday activities with them, without mentioning the self-harming, unless that person chooses to bring it up.
- If the harmer asks you to keep their harming secret, but you think that they are in serious danger, then you must get help for them yourself (either calling for an ambulance, or getting them to see a doctor asap.)

SUICIDE

This is obviously a very serious part of depression and I think it is important to state that just because someone feels depressed, it does not mean they will get suicidal.

However, there will be a few people affected by suicide, or suicidal thoughts, when they are depressed and it is more common in certain groups than in others, though the reason why is unknown.

The majority of people who attempt to commit suicide, thankfully do not die and it is also quite rare to find a child under the age of 14 who wants or has tried to kill themselves. (Usually, if a youngster has killed themselves, it is by accident. Source : www.rcpsych.ac.uk)

However, older teenagers do try to commit suicide and out of 100,000 15-19 year olds, there are 13 suicides. Whether all of these were intentional in causing death, or whether some were only a cry for help that went wrong, we don't know. Young males are more prone to committing suicide in this age group and it tends to occur with those males who have had a previous history of mental illness, have used drugs, abused alcohol, have made previous failed attempts on their lives or they are a relative of a suicide victim.

But what about adults?

What about women?

In an article by Tara Womersley for the Telegraph Group in 2000, she wrote that half of all women 'think of suicide'.

This is a startling statistic if it is a true representation of all women across the globe. In her other statistics, she stated that of 1000 women questioned:

- 41% of women had at one time in their lives, taken anti-depressants
- 17% had phoned The Samaritans for help
- 50% of women comfort ate when they were depressed
- 66% suffered broken nights sleep

Most of the women in the survey (though no exact figure was given) stated that their relationships with their partner were fraught with problems, they had insomnia and sleepless nights over intense money worries.

Add depression to the mix and you can quite clearly see why some women might think of suicide.

But just thinking of suicide does not mean that you will definitely go on to try and take your own life. The thoughts may be all you have. However, The Samaritans report that in 60% of suicides, the victims all consulted their GPs for help, three months prior to taking their own lives.

SOME STATISTICS

- Men are twice as likely to kill themselves as women
- Youths with a crisis over their sexual identity are more likely to commit suicide
- Young Asian women are in a high risk group for suicide (due to racism, socio-economic conditions, future prospects, cultural pressures)
- Unemployed males are more likely to get depressed and consider suicide (Europe)
- Vets, dentists and farmers seem to be in a high risk group (though this is attributed to their proximity to drugs that can be used to precipitate death)
- People who have failed to kill themselves once are at high risk of trying again
- The loss of a much loved spouse and the subsequent grief in bereavement, is a strong motivating factor in the elderly committing suicide
- A history of deliberate, severe self harm increases your risk of committing suicide
- 75% of suicides in the UK are by males

- People suffering with schizophrenia are more at risk of killing themselves
- Females are more likely to commit suicide through overdose (usually paracetemol)

So what can you do if you are worried that someone close to you is perhaps suicidal?

There may or may not be warning signs, but if you are having suspicions, then you must have already, subconsciously or not, picked something up. But usually, there are some definite signs you can be aware of:

- Watch for a definitive change in the person's behaviour. Someone who has suddenly decided to give a lot of their stuff away. They appear numb. Nothing bothers them. They are almost serene. Perhaps they have withdrawn or are refusing to have contact with anyone. They are 'making space' and have difficulty communicating.
- Is the person suddenly expressing huge amounts of distress over their own life? Do they say that they are complete and utter failures? Have they lost all sense of having any self-esteem? Do they seem to be lost? Or have they lost all hope?
- Are they acting like nothing matters? Can they be bothered with anything?
- Are they talking about suicide? Do they seem to be obsessed with death and dying?

Of course, if it was this simple, then anyone would be capable of spotting someone who might be suicidal. Everyone is different and therefore, not everyone who wants to commit suicide will show these signs listed above.

All anyone can do is their best. To look out for their loved ones. Their friends. And be there for one another.

But most importantly, they need to listen.

IS IT A CRY FOR HELP?

In a few cases, attempting to commit suicide, or threatening to commit suicide, is a definite cry for help.

My elder brother once got involved with a girl who had an extremely complicated character, but basically couldn't stand to be on her own. She appeared to have no family and latched onto my brother like a limpet once he showed interest in her. Their relationship got serious very quickly as she declared her love for him and insisted they be together as often as possible. As you might imagine, this became rather stifling after a while and my brother expressed his need to leave the relationship. This girl got very upset and threatened to commit suicide if he did. My brother was very worried. But he knew he couldn't be blackmailed in such a way and truly believed that this girl would not do as she was threatening to.

He left.

She cut her wrists.

But she cut her wrists in a way that would not cause her a lot of harm. There was a lot of blood and mess though. Exactly as she'd planned it, knowing my brother was calling round to see her for a 'chat'. This was her cry for help. And help she got. When she was taken to the hospital, they assigned her to their mental health team and a psychologist saw her before she was discharged.

This woman's pain was 'emotional'. And like any mental disorder, it could not be seen. It wasn't like she had her arm in plaster so that people could see she had broken her arm and might be hurting. All of her pain was 'internal' and this was her only way of letting it out and telling someone.

A person who thinks about, or threatens to, kill themselves, just wants someone who will listen to them. Someone who won't judge what they have to say or constantly interrupt with their own opinions. They want to be able to feel they have someone they can trust to talk to about their problems and sadness.

They want to have someone say that they care.

The most important thing to remember if you're feeling suicidal yourself, is to know that the majority of people who have attempted suicide and failed, usually say to others at a later date, that they are glad that they failed. That they were just after someone to take notice and help. That they didn't want to die they just wanted to stop their pain.

Of course, not every attempt at suicide is a cry for help. Some depressed people really want to die because they feel that it is their only solution to a set of problems that they can see no way out of.

Some will go to great lengths to research ways in which they can kill themselves but for whatever reason, it fails. They do not take enough tablets perhaps, or they are found before they can do themselves enough damage and they are taken to hospital or a doctor.

When a person reaches such a low point, the only way from their can be up. With help from medical professionals and hopefully the love and support of their family (who may have had no idea their family member was feeling this way) can a suicidal person turn their life around.

It won't be a quick journey and it won't be easy. There may have to be a lot of soul searching and a lot of recalling painful events and feelings or trauma.

But they will get there.

With support.

And love.

8

NUTRITION, EXERCISE AND MENTAL HEALTH

Is there a connection between what you put in your mouth and the state of your mental health? And if there is, can your mental health or depressive state be altered by changing the foods you eat?

There have been many studies surrounding food and their various health benefits. We all know we should be eating at least five portions of fruit or vegetables a day. We all know we should drink plenty of water to remain hydrated. We all know which are the 'bad' foods, full of sugar, fat or salt, which we should have only small amounts of occasionally as a treat.

But what about eating specifically to keep your state of mental health balanced?

If you prefer not to take medicines perhaps, then you might like to think there is another approach you could take. Or you might be on antidepressants and also want to give yourself the best chance possible of recovery by eating correctly for mental health?

Whatever your reason, before embarking on any change of diet, you must always consult your doctor beforehand.

Once you have seen your GP, he/she may have given you some advice or diet sheets, but for those who have not been given any information to bring home, listed below, I have included a list of different nutrients, where they can be found, and the benefit on mental health. (This information is also listed at www.mentalhealth.org.uk)

FOR ANXIETY
FOLIC ACID - This can be found in most green, leafy vegetables and is often recommended to pregnant women to be taken in capsule form to help prevent spinal tube defects. It can also be found in some fish, nuts and seeds, beans and pulses, as well as oranges.

MAGNESIUM - This is also found in green vegetables and not just the leafy kind, but also avocados and peppers. Magnesium can also be found in nuts, pulses, wholegrains, legumes such as baked beans, fruit and even chocolate.

FOR POOR CONCENTRATION
VITAMIN B1 - This essential vitamin can be lost in the body through an excessive intake of caffeine and other foods, so it is essential that it be replaced. You can find it in wholegrains, fish and seafood, pork, soya milk, vegetables including mushrooms, aubergine and green peas, lentils, fresh pasta and whole grains.

FOR DEPRESSION
Folic acid and magnesium can help with depression, but also selenium, vitamins C, B6 and B3, zinc, omega 3 fatty acids, tryptophan, tyrosine and GABA. These essential nutrients can

be found in a wide range of different food stuffs such as wholegrains, nuts, meat, seafood and fish, cheeses, fruits and vegetables, beans and pulses, cereals and yeast extracts.

FOR POOR MEMORY
Omega 3 fatty acids found in fish, seeds and nuts are excellent for the brain. Vitamin B12, B6 and B5 are also good nutrients. You can find these in yoghurts, cheese, poached eggs, fish, seafood such as tuna or salmon, wholegrains, fruit and vegetables, pulses and legumes.

FOR IRRITABILITY
Vitamin B6, magnesium and selenium are value foods in helping prevent irritability. They can be found in wholegrains, cereals, nuts, seeds, pulses, legumes, fruits and vegetables, dairy products and chocolate.

FOR STRESS
We all get stressed and what better way to chill out than to prepare ourselves a nice healthy plate of food to help improve our mood? Stress can be alleviated by magnesium, vitamin B3 and vitamin B6. B3 vitamins can be found in wholegrains, vegetables, nuts, fish, seeds and meat such as beef, pork, turkey or chicken.

Please be aware that this is only intended as a guide. You may be allergic to some foods such as shellfish or nuts, and if this is the case then you must source out another type of food that contains the nutrients you need. Above all, you must try and eat a healthy, balanced diet and always, ALWAYS, consult your doctor if you have any worries. Before, during or after. Also, reading this guide, you may be worried that you might not be able to afford some of the foodstuffs, but these meals do not have to be expensive. In a simple dish of pasta, a tin a tuna and some broccoli, you consume an impressive list of vitamin B1, B6, selenium, vitamin B3, B12, omega 3, folic acid, tyrosine, zinc, magnesium, vitamin C and B5.

Or what about an egg with some baked beans? That alone gives you magnesium, vitamin B12, zinc, tryptophan and selenium!

As you can see, a healthy, nutrition-rich diet need not be an expensive one.

And it's not just what you eat that can have a significant impact on the state of your mental health.

Exercise has also been proven to be an effective treatment for those suffering with mild depression, anxiety or stress. Your doctor can even 'prescribe' you exercise therapy as part of your treatment.

The Mental Health Foundation is trying to promote the beneficial effects of exercise on conditions like depression and the three main aims of their campaign are:

- To increase the amount of doctors who prescribe exercise referral schemes to patients suffering with mild to moderate depression
- To raise awareness in the general public and the medical professions, about the fact that performing physical exercise regularly, is one of the most effective ways to help look after, if not improve, mental health

■ To raise awareness about the importance of finding and using effective ways to treat anyone suffering with any kind of depression

Their Exercise and Depression Campaign is an important move by the Mental Health Foundation. But essentially, it is a beneficial fact-finding one.

Exercise has already been proven to:

■ Lift/change mood
■ Reduce feelings of anxiety
■ Improve a person's feelings of self-esteem
■ Improve concentration and memory
■ Increases the release of the 'feel-good' endorphins in the body
■ Gets a person active and removed from isolation
■ Gives a person a reason to set themselves goals

From what we know about depression, these reasons would be extremely beneficial to anyone living with depression. We already know how isolated and numb you can become. We already know how unmotivated and hopeless about the future you can feel. Getting out and about, exercising, can make someone feel better about themselves. Give themselves a routine for each day and a goal to reach and then the feel-good factor when they achieve those goals, no matter how large or small they may be. During exercise, it also gives you the chance to meet other like-minded people and increases your circle of friends, reducing isolation, whether you go to a gym every day or just run in the local park. And exercise can be something as cheap and simple as just going for a brisk walk. Increasing your heartbeat for thirty minutes or more is an excellent way to improve the health and stamina in your body.

And not just physically.

We have to realise that it's not just physical injury that can damage a body. You don't have to have a broken bone or a diseased lung to inflict damage upon your body.

A paper published in the medical journal, 'The Lancet', stated that if a person suffers with depression, then the mental condition can damage/inflict a person's health to a greater degree than many other long-term physical diseases such as angina, arthritis, asthma and diabetes. (The paper was written after results from a World Health Organisation poll of over a quarter of a million people worldwide.)

A significant fact, I think you'll agree, and one that not many people will realise.

WHAT ELSE CAN I DO TO HELP MYSELF?

Helping yourself when you have depression can be a very proactive situation. For some, it may be hard to do, especially if they are feeling lethargic, unmotivated and numb. But alongside the help you will receive from the GP, you can also help yourself with some simple techniques and ideas that will work brilliantly alongside any medication you are taking. (Remember that you must always consult your doctor if you think you have depression. Self-help ideas are not alternatives to seeing your doctor.)

First of all, your doctor can give you information on local self-help groups, or you could contact the Depression Alliance or the Mental Health Foundation who may be able to put you in touch with local groups in your area, of other people who are working to rid themselves of depression or other mental health conditions. Sharing experiences, histories and stories with others in a similar condition as you, can be a very strengthening, bonding experience. It helps reduce feelings of isolation and helps you realise that you aren't alone in this. There are others out there suffering too. Who knows, just by being there and lending an ear to someone else, you might help them too and just that simple fact might help make you feel better. Like you are making a beneficial contribution to someone else's life.

But what if self-help groups aren't for you? What if you don't feel like sitting in a strange room with a bunch of strangers? Well, there are correspondence schemes, too and pen-pal initiatives. These can be just as helpful to a sufferer of depression as some people feel they can put their feelings down better on paper, knowing they aren't going to be interrupted.

Another way to help yourself, is to gather information on your condition. Reading this book is an excellent example! But learning more about your condition can reduce anxiety or even fear about it. We all fear what we don't know and knowledge is definitely power. The Depression Alliance have a recommended reading list if you'd like a good book, but there are also many leaflets you could pick up, or videos/DVDs from your local library. You could even use their computers to access the internet if you wish. Many libraries run Silver Surfer classes for those that are older and don't have much experience or confidence using a computer. So don't let that aspect put you off.

Relaxing is another great way to help with your

condition. Some sufferers of depression can feel tense, wound up or agitated. Learning to relax, by taking out ten minutes of every day to sit and breathe/listen to some mood music/do yoga/t'ai chi/pilates or even give yourself a short weekend break if you can afford it, can work wonders. So many of us forget the need to just simply relax and quite frankly, everyone could benefit from doing this each day. Taking a moment to concentrate on our breathing, lower our blood pressure and stress levels and try not to think of anything.

Just breathe.

Exercise we know can also help us feel more positive about life, as can changing what we eat, but another thing you can do to help yourself is to pursue your hobbies and interests. Make an effort to find that one thing that you absolutely adore doing and do it!

9

BEREAVEMENT AND DEPRESSION

Everybody, at some point in their lives, are going to be bereaved. This death can be of a parent, or child, or a family friend, and it is such a terrible shock and upset to our lives, that it can definitely lead to cases of depression in some people.

Obviously, death is not something we can prepare for, even if we know that someone is suffering from a terminal illness and we have 'time' to 'get used to' the idea of losing that person. When death does come, it can still be a great shock, even if we can comfort ourselves in that the person who has died is no longer suffering and is now at peace.

NORMAL REACTIONS TO BEREAVEMENT

- Shock
- Denial
- Feeling numb
- Stunned/dazed
- Lack of appetite
- Exhaustion
- Insomnia/sleep too much
- Fear
- Guilt
- Depression

Reading through this list (excepting the last) you can see that a lot of the symptoms are ones that would be produced if you suffered from depression. So the range of healthy, normal reactions to death should not always be confused with depression. It is when this state of affairs continues in a person that they feel they just cannot move on and are bogged down in their feelings of grief, that depression becomes a real threat.

After the initial shock of bereavement, and the first few days have passed by, those left behind may feel that they need to search for answers to 'rationalise' the death of their loved one. Sometimes, this search for answers can make a bereaved person act in the strangest of ways. Sufferers may be angry, and rant and rage or pull places apart as they search for a particular document or keepsake. They may suddenly feel the need to scream at someone in their need for answers to fully understand what occurred and why.

It is incredibly important to be able to vent grief. Feelings, no matter what they are, when held in and kept restrained behind a mask, can cause a lot of physical, never mind mental, problems. People who are unable to express themselves are more likely to feel isolated and numb and this, as we know, can also be an effect of depression.

Bereaved people should never be made to feel ashamed or embarrassed about their feelings or reactions or what they might say at this time. This searching for answers is normal. It is part of the grieving process, of which there is a recognised stage.

The next stage to occur, is usually a sensation of feeling disorientated or disorganised in some way. That for some reason, they just cannot get a grip on what is happening in the world. A person may feel they lack control or motivation to get through their day. They may just want to sit on the sofa or curl up in a bed, because that is just the easiest thing to do. Why interact with people and the world when nothing seems to go right anyway? What can they trust? Their judgement? They're not sure. The best thing to do during this stage if you know someone who has been bereaved, is to listen. Listening to someone who needs to express how they feel, or the questions they have, or the emotions rampaging through them, will be a healthier individual at the end of the process. The world may seem to lack rules at that time to them, but at least they've got someone they can talk to.

If you know of someone who has experienced a death, never expect them to get over it quickly, even if they appear to be doing so. Death is a major life event amongst humans and no matter how often someone may tell you that they aren't that bothered or upset that someone close to them has died, they will be denying their own feelings. Just make sure that you are there for them when they do eventually need someone to talk to. Strong characters especially may feel that they are not allowed to show 'weakness' by grieving and may secretly be struggling with everything that is going off inside whilst presenting a mask to the world.

Let them know that you are there. Let them know that you will always be happy to be a listening ear when they need one and that whatever they say will be confidential and never repeated to anyone else.

Guilt at moving on with life afterwards, can be a major point at which depression can take hold. After weeks and months of struggling with a death, knowing that you have to move on can cause these feelings of guilt. Sufferers believe that they are ready to start to want to move on, but worry about what everyone else may think. They might not be able to adapt to what has been lost to them and find that this 'handicap' is ruining their work or private life.

Death always makes people reassess their own lives and it is at this stage that people can make some major decisions about their own lives which can be either exciting or terrifying. They may wonder if their judgement is impaired and second guess themselves. This may even become so bad, their self-esteem is so low that they may ultimately become depressed. Wanting to make changes, but unable to move forward on their own.

CHILDREN AND DEATH

Adults can understand that there is life and death in the universe, but children, especially very young children, may have great difficulties in dealing with death and bereavement. They may know the word, but when it comes to really understanding what it means, can be a different process entirely.

Some children may cry and be upset, but don't be worried if your child does not consistently cry for many days the way an adult might. As some children can get through grief very quickly. They may experience the initial upset. Cry. Feel sad. Feel a little bewildered. But then they might be ready to just carry on with life, being happy just to remember the deceased during happy times, or by looking at photos and saying, "do you remember…..?"

Sometimes, all a child needs when they are grieving is a cuddle. To be held and comforted by someone they trust.

Never tell a child they 'mustn't be upset'. Never tell them they shouldn't cry or how they should be feeling. Allow a child to work through grief the way they need to. If they ask lots of questions, then try as best as you can to answer them, to an age appropriate level. And be patient if you hear those questions more than once!

Another good thing to do when a child has lost someone they loved, is to try and maintain order and stability in that child's life. Obviously if they need a couple of days or a week off school initially, then do it, but the quicker they are returned to normal and see that the world continues to carry on, the better.

And when the moments come long into the future where that child has a better understanding of death and has even more questions, then continue to answer them. Children may get through the stages of grief quickly, but the effects of death last a lifetime.

10

USEFUL ADDRESSES

Below is a generalised list of useful sites and addresses that anyone can take advantage of. Most helplines are 24 hours, but those that are not have their times set alongside. Regarding websites, I have only recommended those that I feel are reliable and dependable, but I cannot be responsible for any of their third party information and/or links to other sites. I have also included those that are US or Australian based, as they include some very helpful information that would be of importance to anyone affected by a mental health condition.

www.samaritans.org

24 hour helpline
UK 08457 90 90 90
ROI 1850 60 90 90
Jo@samaritans.org

(The Samaritans provide a confidential helpline and advice centre and the website provides links to local branches, gives information on volunteering/training to be a samaritan, as well as general, helpful information.)

www.rcpsych.ac.uk
(The website for the Royal College of Psychiatrists. This site gives a lot of helpful information to the layperson.)

www.netdoctor.co.uk/depression/index.shtml
(This UK site is filled with comprehensive information about depression, the different types of depression, the social aspects, diagnosing depression, medicines and treatments, alternative treatments, talking therapies and individual case histories. An easy site to navigate.)

www.depressionalliance.org/
(This site is not associated with the registered charity Depression Alliance [no: 1096741]. This site provides much information to the general public regarding publications about depression, raising money and awareness for the condition.)

www.mind.org.uk
(The site for the National Association for Mental Health. This easy to navigate site has lots of information for the many different mental health conditions.)

www.phobics-society.org.uk/
(The site for the National Phobics Society. It has lots of information on anxiety, phobia and depression. It also runs a helpline that is open Monday to Friday from 9.15am - 9.00pm. 0870 122 2325. You can also email them at info@phobics-society.org.uk)

www.crusebereavementcare.org.uk/
(This site helps you find your local branch of Cruse and also provides online information on how to cope with a crisis or loss. They run two helplines, one for adults and one for children. The helplines are open Monday to Friday 9.30am - 5.00pm for adults at 0844 477 9400. The Young Person's Free Phone Helpline is at 0808 808 1677. They also can be contacted via email at info@rd4u.org.uk)

www.pni.org.uk
(This site is for women suffering from post-natal Illness and post-natal depression. Registered Charity no : 1113840)

www.nhsdirect.nhs.uk
(This site is run by the NHS and offers health information for all conditions including depression and other mental health issues.)

www.bacp.co.uk
(This site is for the British Association of Counselling and Psychotherapy. An excellent site, you can use it to find a local registered therapist in your area, give information about education and training, latest news in research and information.)

www.ccyp.co.uk
(This site is about Counselling Children and Young People.)

www.bma.org.uk
(The site for the British Medical Association.)

www.bully-off.co.uk
(This site offers a complete guide to stamping out bullying for good and what children can do to help themselves.)

www.alcoholconcern.org.uk
Waterbridge House,
32-36 Loman Street,
London SE1 0EE.
(This site is run by Alcohol Concern, providing information and a helpline. 020 7928 7377)

www.childline.org.uk
Headquarters
Studd Street,
London
N1 0QW

www.redundancyhelp.co.uk/counselling.html
(A site providing information and support to those who have been made redundant.)

www.sane.org.uk
(A site dedicated to mental health, providing information and support. Their helpline is on 0845 767 8000)

www.youngminds.org.uk
(This site is run by a mental health charity specifically aimed at young people under the age of eighteen.)

www.mummysblue.co.uk
(Support and advice for women and their families trying to cope with post natal depression and illness.)

www.depressionafterdelivery.com
Depression After Delivery Incorporated
91 East Somerset Street
Raritan
NJ 08869

www.psychologyinfo.com/depression
(Site filled with information about the different types of depression with separate sections for teenagers, seniors and women.)

www.mentalhealthshop.org
(Site filled with resources about depression - leaflets, books, videos, DVDs, etc.)

www.beyondblue.org.au
(Australian site, filled with information about the symptoms of depression, how to help friends and family members, research, anxiety, bipolar, post-natal depression and an information line [1300 22 4636])

www.kidshealth.org
(Great site with lots of information on children's health, not just depression, but all aspects that might affect youngsters.)

www.bipolar.com
(A US site, with lots of relative information about bipolar depression, what it actually is, the different treatment options, living with bipolar and how family and friends can help.)

www.depression-guide.com
(A site providing an alphabetical listing of Mental Health Disorders.)

www.sada.org.uk
Seasonal Affective Disorder Association
PO Box 989
Steyning
BN44 3HG

THE HELPLINES
Samaritans
UK 08457 90 90 90
ROI 850 60 90 90

Beyond Blue (Australia)
1300 22 4636

National Phobics Society
0870 122 2325
(Monday to Friday 9.15am - 9.00pm)

Cruse Bereavement
0844 477 9400 (Adults)
0808 808 1677 (Young Person's Free Phone Helpline)

Alcohol Concern
020 7928 7377

Saneline
0845 767 8000

AUTHORS ACKNOWLEDGEMENTS

I would like to thank all of those that shared their stories with me on either a confidential basis or with the intention of having their experience included in this book. I would specifically like to thank my mother, Doreen Nicholson, for providing insights never shared before and daily phone conversations, where we were able to put the world to rights! I would also like to thank my children for letting mummy get on with her work without creating too many interruptions. And finally, I would like to acknowledge all of those people out there, who continue to struggle with depression day in and day out, with or without help and their families who try to support them. The stigma of depression and mental health issues still remains in some places and until this barrier to understanding is removed, we will not be able to get help to all the people who need it.

Index

Emerald Publishing
www.emeraldpublishing.co.uk

106 Ladysmith Road
Brighton BN2 4EG

Other titles in the Emerald Series:

Law
Guide to Bankruptcy
Conducting Your Own Court case
Guide to Consumer law
Creating a Will
Guide to Family Law
Guide to Employment Law
Guide to European Union Law
Guide to Health and Safety Law
Guide to Criminal Law
Guide to Landlord and Tenant Law
Guide to the English Legal System
Guide to Housing Law
Guide to Marriage and Divorce
Guide to The Civil Partnerships Act
Guide to The Law of Contract
The Path to Justice
You and Your Legal Rights

Health
Guide to Combating Child Obesity
Asthma Begins at Home

Music
How to Survive and Succeed in the Music Industry

General
A Practical Guide to Obtaining probate
A Practical Guide to Residential Conveyancing
Writing The Perfect CV
Keeping Books and Accounts-A Small Business Guide
Business Start Up-A Guide for New Business
Finding Asperger Syndrome in the Family-A Book of Answers
A Guide to Dementia Care
For details of the above titles published by Emerald go to:

www.emeraldpublishing.co.uk